AN ONWARD JOURNEY

A STORY OF LOVE, PERSEVERANCE & FAITH

KARTAR CHAND

Copyright © 2020 by Kartar Chand

All rights reserved. No part of this publication may be reproduced, distributed, or transmitted in any form or by any means, including photocopying, recording, or other electronic or mechanical methods, without the prior written permission of the publisher, except in the case of brief quotations embodied in critical reviews and certain other noncommercial uses permitted by copyright law. For permission requests, email "Attention: Permissions," at the email below.

For copyright reasons, I have changed the names of some of the participants in my life.

AN ONWARD JOURNEY
A Story of Love, Perseverance & Faith

Kartar Chand
anonwardjourney@gmail.com

Copyright ©2020
ISBN 978-1-943343-13-3 PB | 978-1-943343-17-1 CB

Printed in the United States of America

DestinedToPublish.com 773.783.2981

Dedicated
to the loving memory
of my
beloved wife
and my dear parents
who are no more

AN ONWARD JOURNEY

ACKNOWLEDGMENTS

First, my special thanks to my daughter, the late Raksha Devi, who inspired me with her wisdom and thoughts. She was the first person who encouraged me to write an autobiography.

This autobiography also owes its completion to the extensive involvement of some of my grandchildren, particularly Neena, who typed the manuscript. She gave considerable energy and enthusiasm to this time-consuming and daunting task. My book could never have been written without your support. I am especially grateful for my granddaughter Anita for her willingness to read the manuscript with the painstaking care and sensitive understanding that only she can provide. I wish to thank my eldest daughter Kamlesh, who read the chapters and suggested vital improvements. Also, my sincere thanks to my granddaughter Sonia for her interest in my written memoirs.

My thanks go to all who encouraged me to write this book and to all the others who helped bring it into being. Again, I thank Anita, Neena, Sonia, Vik, my children, and others for inspiring me to become a writer. I am truly blessed to have them as my family.

Further, I want to thank the staff at the local library on Layton Avenue in Milwaukee for their kind attention and help finding books that suit my interests. I also extend my thanks to the staff of the Barnes and Noble on South Seventy-Sixth Street in Milwaukee, Wisconsin, for accommodating me in my search for books and journals.

Finally, I offer special thanks to Destined To Publish, to Marilyn Alexander, and to the editor, Hannah, for her brief but strong note of encouragement. It was an unexpected and delightful surprise and I gained a lot of inspiration; a new, enriched power; and an enhanced sense of satisfaction in my writing from this letter. It means more to me than you will ever know.

Lastly, I would like to thank the late Shiv Raj, a great friend and close relative, for being such a great source of support in my lifelong struggle for liberty and survival.

Kartar Chand

FOREWORD

It is difficult to imagine being born in a world that does not appreciate you or your potential, does not see you as equal to others around you. Furthermore, being born in a country under foreign rule, and one that suffers from deeply rooted caste discrimination. My grandfather's frustration and heartache were constant as this was his world during much of his life.

Throughout my life, he has shared many stories with me and my family about his struggles. These captivating accounts describe in vivid detail places, people, and emotions he went through that made an impact on his life; rich experiences that most of us couldn't fathom today. His core values and moral principles compelled him to embark on a remarkable life journey that enabled a more fulfilling, safer life for his children. A courageous story of faith and resilience that has influenced many, especially me. He ultimately paved the path to freedom, and because of that, I will always have the utmost gratitude, love, and respect for him.

Considering all of the sacrifices my grandfather made for his family, I am humbled to simply be in the

United States, the land of the free, because of him. Quality healthcare, education, technology, and even just clean, breathable air are examples of seemingly simple characteristics of the country that are in fact inaccessible in other parts of the world. Moreover, we have constitutionally guaranteed rights such as my grandfather's right to speak his mind and write this book, yet another achievement which may have been impossible and even denounced back home.

His stories teach us not to take this country for granted and to embrace its foundational ideals such as liberty, equality, and opportunity - freedoms that were not easily granted, and for which not only have our fallen heroes made the ultimate sacrifice, but immigrants flee their motherlands to seek.

Just as my grandfather's life has been an extraordinary journey, authoring his life story was also a tremendous commitment that started many years ago, and I am so proud that he is now sharing it with the world. My hope is that by reading his memoirs, he will have also influenced you to take advantage of opportunity, follow your heart and take that leap of faith, always be kind and respectful to others, and always remember those in your life that have helped you along your journey, just as he did.

Anita

CONTENTS

Introduction ix

PART I

Chapter 1	Casteism and Brahmanism 1
Chapter 2	Attainments and Aspirations 7
Chapter 3	Parentage & Birth 15
Chapter 4	Childhood & Youth 27
Chapter 5	Primary School 37
Chapter 6	My Village 41
Chapter 7	High School 55
Chapter 8	Shiv Raj 61
Chapter 9	My Visit to Shimla 68
Chapter 10	Our Wedding 74
Chapter 11	Nasib Kaur and Her Setbacks 81
Chapter 12	My Helplessness 86
Chapter 13	August 15, 1947 91
Chapter 14	Mohat Ram: Man, of Goodwill and Ill Will 100
Chapter 15	My College Years 109

CHAPTER 16	A Dreadful Night	117
CHAPTER 17	Religion	123
CHAPTER 18	Pride & Prejudice	127
CHAPTER 19	The Struggle for a Passport	138
CHAPTER 20	A Parent's Dilemma	144

PART II

CHAPTER 21	Preparation for the United Kingdom	151
CHAPTER 22	My Journey to the Unknown	159
CHAPTER 23	The Best Gift from My Father	174
CHAPTER 24	Our New Life in Scotland	178
CHAPTER 25	Education & Training in Scotland	191
CHAPTER 26	Charen Ginda	202
CHAPTER 27	My Return Visit to India	207
CHAPTER 28	The National Leather Sellers College London	214
CHAPTER 29	The Clyde Leather Company	223
CHAPTER 30	Beverley, Yorkshire	229
CHAPTER 31	The United States	238
CHAPTER 32	My Wife's Visit to India	245
CHAPTER 33	Big Changes and Choices	252
CHAPTER 34	Nasib Kaur's Return to India	260
CHAPTER 35	Dedications and Disappointments	265
CHAPTER 36	After Retirement	272
CHAPTER 37	My Dreams and Unfulfilled Dreams	279
Selected Bibliography		285
End Notes		289

INTRODUCTION

Since I left my home country of India in 1954, the urge to write my memoirs had overtaken me. I was disadvantaged in that I lacked the English vocabulary and diction to produce a narrative that would be readable, coherent, and lucid. At the same time, I was impeded by insufficient free time and overpowered by strong convictions, personal responsibilities, and commitment to my family. Centuries-old Indian myths that only the rich and royal, poets and padres, scholars and Sufis could write their autobiographies clouded my mind for a long time.

The real awakening for me to write my memoirs occurred when my daughters were in primary school in Glasgow, Scotland. They sometimes asked me about my parents and ancestors, hoping to make a family tree like their Scottish friends were doing in school. I was speechless for a while because they were quite right for asking questions and I was quite wrong for not answering and not knowing much about my ancestors. Laughing, I told my daughters that I knew about a Christmas tree, but I'd never heard of a family tree. I didn't want to create any negative feelings or an inferiority complex in the young minds of my innocent kids; I wanted them to grow up as carefree children. However, their questions floated through my mind day and night, and I felt that I had to fulfill the promises I had made to them. They wanted to know who they were and what their heritage was.

At the same time, the intense feeling grew every day, telling me that I must provide some comfort and food for reflection for my children, grandchildren, and great-grandchildren. I want to leave some type of record of my life and family. But more than that, I want to bring out all kinds of things that have been buried deep in my heart for a long time. I want to tell the stories of my complicated life of misery, struggle, and throbbing pain.

All these years, I've been reluctant to talk about my ordeal, and to this day, my children don't even fully understand my life experiences. I have nothing to brag about regarding my heritage. My parents and grandparents were not ministers to the Nawabs or Maharajas, nor were they owners of half of India or religious Brahman priests. Like many in India, I wasn't born with a silver spoon in my mouth and my parents had no mansion or palace. Despite that, I'm very proud to say that my parents were hardworking, simple, humble, and happy people. They were God-fearing, generous, and tended to be religious. They were good human beings.

I am truly blessed to be here in America, a great country indeed, where I've found a new sense of confidence, exhilaration, and inspiration, a new determination to achieve freedom and human dignity. Upon stepping foot in America, I realized quickly that I could do what I wanted and take advantage of any opportunities along the way. This was an important turning point in my life.

After retiring from my job and losing my beloved wife in September 2005, writing about my past became my primary occupation, a necessary one during the long solitude of a lonely life. I wanted to leave a legacy—the legacy of centuries of neglect and suffering. To do that, I realized that I should put everything into words. It had become unrelenting torture for me not to tell the story of my traumatic life experiences. There are lots of ups and downs in everyone's lives, but I suffered a lot of downs inflicted by the society I lived in for the best part of my life, resulting in smoldering rage and frustration. Again, a writer is a custodian of all his memories, and memories too often die with the owner. Time often runs out to narrate one's deepest thoughts and feelings about life. Considering all these factors, I've attempted in these pages to narrate the events as I saw them. I feel it's important that the truth be told.

This book is based on compelling real-life experiences that I survived with persistent effort and courage and my desire to offer hope to others. This narrative reveals the inhumanity of caste Brahmans, based on old, firmly held beliefs and opinions, to starve the poor. It gives an overview of my life and its achievements, a life I lived with courage and conviction. I was never deterred and found a lot of purpose in my life. These are all inspiring, extraordinary untold stories of survival and resilience. Finally, the entire narrative is a story of the constant struggle to make a decent living and free myself, my family, and future generations from evil.

I'm confident that nothing I've written bears a trace of ill will against any society or individual as I muster enough courage to tell them the truth. At the same time, I believe that relating all these incidents and connected accounts will, without a doubt, benefit my readers. Hopefully, it will make a difference in their lives by providing a quick dose of hope and inspiration. In a nutshell, this book is about courage, conviction, and perseverance.

It is my hope that this book will give readers a deep understanding of the critical issues and an appreciation of complex but seemingly simple issues. I want to acquaint the reader with my faults and errors, and at the same time, I want the reader to think about the enigmatic Indian society that lost its morality and humanity, destroyed the brotherhood of a nation, and tarnished the image of our motherland through segregation and bigotry. In these deeply moving and unforgettable memoirs, I have described my odyssey from anger and isolation to forgiveness and activism. I have also criticized individuals and groups, sometimes rather severely, which was unavoidable and necessary. This criticism doesn't take away my respect for many of them.

PART I

CHAPTER ONE

CASTEISM AND BRAHMANISM

First, a few words need to be said about casteism and Brahmanism for non-Indian readers because these two words are the bone of contention, the ideas responsible for all India's troubles, and no one in the world has managed to diagnose this stupid, horrible manmade disease.

The Indian caste system is incredibly complex and describing it in detail is beyond the scope of this book. Distinguished scholars and historians have written large volumes on the subject. My humble intention is to provide readers a very concise and emotive narrative of casteism and Brahmanism, their effect on me, and what they did to the millions of poor and innocent people who became their victims. These cancerous diseases have caused suffering, humiliation, degradation, and deprivation for centuries, and people are still suffering all over India. One can tolerate natural calamities, but it's very difficult and painful to suffer due to a manmade, barbarous misery created by one's own unscrupulous, ignorant, and greedy countrymen, in this case the Brahmans and their Brahmanism and fascism.

The Indian caste system is an essential part of

AN ONWARD JOURNEY

Hinduism and traditional Hindu life is organized around it. It's not very familiar to the rest of the world. The system enforces the superiority of the Hindu Brahman priests and the inferiority of the poor and oppressed. Castes decide the family structure and family occupations of the poor. They decide one's position in life. In brief, castes control the lives of millions of poor untouchables and have made them suffer for centuries. Why? Because the main motive of the Brahmans is to make poor people and untouchables their slaves. They want them to follow their will. They exploit them and deprive them of basic rights like education and knowledge throughout their lives. It's against basic humanitarian values to enslave humanity this way and has no parallel in the entire world.

Who were these Brahmans? According to historians, they descended from Aryans, foreigners who invaded northwest India during the prehistoric period. The Aryans came to India from a remote Russian valley in central Asia. The indigenous people, namely the Kohls, Dravidians, Mongolians racial type and aboriginal tribes occupied the land then. They were primitive, dark-skinned people with broad noses who lived as forest dwellers, hunters, and fishermen. Aryans were tall, fair-skinned, arrogant, shrewd, tough warrior people. They infiltrated northwest India and overthrew or killed the Indus valley dwellers, settling along the banks of the Indus river and in Punjab. They left behind a vivid picture of themselves in their early literature, the Vedas. These writings have given their name to this period of Aryan India, known as Vedic India. There were four Vedas, but the most important was the Rig Veda. Later, other works were added to the original Vedas by Brahman writers and acquired their sacred status.

AN ONWARD JOURNEY

Vedic Aryans brought their gods and culture with them. There was no ban on the consumption of food cooked by the Sudras and the food was not considered polluted by the touch of a lower caste member as there was no caste system in the Rig Veda.[1] Animal sacrifices were offered. The cow was treated as a normal animal; there was no traditional veneration of cattle, and the cow was not considered the mother of Vedic Aryans. Intoxicating spirits were freely consumed by the original Aryans.[2] Cow, buffalo, and horse meat were freely eaten by these Aryans. In other words, the forefathers of the Hindu Brahmans ate cow meat and anything else Europeans ate. Nothing was sacred to them. Aryans came from very cold countries and meat was indeed the best kind of food for them.

From Vedic India, we come to the Indian epic period. This time is named after the two great epic poems, the Ramayana and Mahabharata. These works have become a kind of collection of Hindu ideas in the hands of a long succession of Hindu Brahman editors. Over time, these editors converted the simple adventure stories into books of devotion for their own benefit, and the pictures illustrating the two epics differ greatly from those of Vedic India. They changed even the language, Sanskrit, from a flexible tongue to a complex language.

By the time the Aryans moved further east toward Bihar, they were no longer pure Aryan tribes. They married local women because they hadn't brought many women with them. There has been a radical religious change since Vedic times. The old Vedic gods were superseded by the new great gods of the Hindu Brahmans: Vishnu, Shiva, Brahma, etc. Other gods were introduced, some in animal form like Ganesh, the elephant head, and Hanuman, the monkey. With the new gods came new ideas. The idea of the incarnation of a god in human form (avatar), absent from the Rig Veda, was established and both Rama and Krishna represent incarnations of Vishnu.[2] Along with this came the doctrine of karma, dharma, etc. Socially and politically, other great changes took place. The institution of castes, one of the cornerstones of Hinduism, appeared. In the Rig Veda, there were four orders of society. Now there are many segregated groups, and the Hinduism of the land developed a characteristic culture of its own called Brahmanism, "a veritable chamber of horrors," as Dr. Ambedkar once said.

The Hindus divided society into four castes: Brahman, Kshatriya, Vaishya, and Shudra. The Brahman's duty was to study and teach religion and perform rituals and sacrifices. The Kshatriyas fought wars and ruled the country, the Vaishyas were tradesmen, and the Shudras served the first three castes as laborers. All those outside these four orders were untouchables. Untouchables were confined to the tasks other Hindu caste members didn't like, like street cleaning, farming, scavenging, tanning, weaving, hunting, and fishing. A long-oppressed ethnic group among Hindus, untouchables are called Hindus for political purposes, like vote counting, but they've never been recognized by the Hindus as brethren.

Louis Fischer, an eminent writer, writes that an untouchable is exactly that: he or she must not touch a caste Hindu or anything a caste Hindu touches. They're barred from entering a Hindu temple, home, or shop. In villages, untouchables were forced to live on the lowest outskirts, into which dirty water drained. In cities, they inhabited the worst neighborhoods (slums) and weren't allowed to go to schools but remained illiterate. On the other hand, someone said correctly that the untouchables are the saviors of the Brahmans (dodgers). They've suffered for centuries in the country of the dodgers. They're the real people who feed the dodger and keep him alive. They've worked hard all their lives and are taken for granted and left to decay.

As time passed, the power and prestige of the Brahmans increased immensely. The Brahman priests claimed to be gods on earth. They became master manipulators. They became con artists. They became corrupted. They became callous brutes and believed in rogue justice. They betrayed every essential human principle in order to establish their system of power. Their deeds were uncivilized. They designed the system to crush the very life out of the untouchable poor and benefit themselves.

Brahman priests have done more harm than good to the country and society over these thousands of years. They've made India a nation of slaves. Racism is deeply ingrained in them. They forced the segregation of racial minorities, causing a rift in the country. They created a literal depression in poor untouchable communities. They stopped the country's progress by denying others education. They divided the country with caste prejudice. They made India a dangerous place to be a woman or poor. They were unproductive and became high-class predators by brainwashing the uneducated poor with their myths and mumbo-jumbo, then lived on them for centuries. For centuries, the Brahmans have worked for their own interests, not for other societies. They've become addicted to their power. This addiction has no end; it goes on forever.

Other sections of society, like the Muslims and Sikhs, have followed the Hindu Brahmans in practicing social distinction and inequality, but over time, many of them have improved with the help of education, understanding, and communication. It's wrong to think that all Brahmans, Banias, Sikhs, and Muslims are bad. I have lot of good cultured friends from different parts of society. Only a small percentage are bad, those who possess an orthodox, radical, or fanatical character and are dangerous to the poor and the country. Unless this bad group is stabilized and humanized, India will keep suffering. Again, I have used the word *evil* many times in this book, and this word applies only to bad groups or people who are trying to destroy the country, who oppose humanity, try to rob the poor and live on them, and have no conscience.

CHAPTER TWO

ATTAINMENTS AND ASPIRATIONS

There was a time when my life seemed unimaginably painful in my hometown in India. I was baffled by my own life. My young mind was impacted by the caste system and by the so-called "high-caste people" and their barbaric customs and traditions. Civility and decency were nowhere to be found. To put it into a different perspective, the high-caste people had no conscience. They had no fear of God and they did evil things to those of the lower or poorer castes. Even today, caste distinction remains embedded in their blood. Many of those in the upper caste are still blind and static due to the snobbery of caste placement.

Time changes, wind changes, weather changes, but the ignorance of those who consider themselves part of a "super-caste" has never changed. They know nothing about humanism. The unfortunate fact is that people in the higher castes are guilty for everything they've done to the poor in the eyes of God. They were not superior people or even close to superior, as they pretended all the time. As stated by Reverend Desmond Tutu, archbishop of Cape Town, "when they dehumanized other people by inflicting pain and suffering on them, they dehumanized themselves."³ This fact is beyond the understanding of the Indian Brahman priests and their fellow oppressors. The poor have kept on surviving despite the evils that have brought them so much suffering and misery through the centuries.

This is history for me now, but sometimes it's worthwhile to remember the past in order to better appreciate the present quality of life. Good sense and hard work paid off, and now, by the grace of God, I'm living happily in America. God must have heard my prayers and I couldn't ask for more.

GAINED HEALTH
Once while growing up in India, at age twenty-one, I became sick and lost a lot of weight. I envisioned that I wouldn't live to see forty years of age. By the grace of God, I'm here in good health. I celebrated my eighty-eighth birthday with great pomp and I'm still going strong. Every day is a blessing for me.

Another example of God's grace occurred with my wife's eyesight. She almost went blind at the age of eighteen and had struggled with poor vision for much of her life. In India, there was no competent eye doctor, so we wasted several years and lots of money chasing after phony doctors there. When she came to Scotland in 1955, her eyesight was restored, and she was relieved to be able to see again. Health is everything. Health is really a great wealth, and here I have acquired all the wealth I ever wanted.

GAINED FULL FREEDOM
During my school years in India, I suffered miserably at the hands of the unscrupulous society and

schoolteachers because of bigotry and discrimination. I was striving hard to learn, but the teachers made it extremely difficult for me. In India, I was bogged down, hedged in, and bound inside my mind and body. I ceased to breathe freely and felt that I was suffocating. My own compatriots called themselves superior, and they humiliated and betrayed me because I was part of a different caste, but the American people love me and respect me. My own fellow citizens put me down and destroyed the best part of my life, but Americans elevate me to where I want to be. Indian people made me angry, but Americans make me happy. This behavior was disgusting and shameful of the Indian people. But today, in America, I'm free. I move freely. I talk about whatever I want to freely, which was impossible in India and never will be if caste prejudice exists and children in Indian society continue to be educated this way. Truly, America has made me proud and I hold my head high. This has made a big difference in my life.

To date, I've acquired the education I need and I'm thriving and surviving. My children and grandchildren are studying at well-known universities all over America and the sky is the limit for them.

What I wanted to achieve during all those years in India was simple happiness and satisfaction. These things were hard to come by under the tyranny of so-called Brahmanism, under Sikhs, Muslims, and other high-caste people. I've struggled mightily to reach this point. Perhaps it's the struggle that gives value to life. Life is full of ups and downs, and I've faced all kinds of obstacles in India due to caste discrimination. But by the grace of God, I've seen no barricades here. I can live the way I want and do what I want, and I've managed to succeed.

AN ONWARD JOURNEY

FULFILLED MY DREAMS AND SAW THE WORLD

When I was young, I was very passionate about seeing important natural and historical places—a dream that remained with me until I came to America. This great country has offered me ample opportunities to travel throughout the world and see the beauty of nature and the hard work of poor people. Now it seems that my hard struggle has paid off and life seems enriched by every perspective.

Up to the age of fourteen, I felt more like a prisoner in my small village because I was outspoken about caste and wrong traditions, and thus my father was always worried about my safety. In 1945, my relative Shiv Raj invited me to go to Shimla, a popular summer resort.

This was a real turning point in my life. Shimla showed me a different environment. Its population was mainly British, and it felt as if there was freedom from the usual aura of the caste system. There, I visited surrounding villages like Chotta Shimla, Jutogh, and Jakhu Hill, and was fascinated by the surrounding deodar trees, snow-capped Himalayan mountains, and evergreen valleys, which were all new to me. There was no danger in roaming through the dense trees. I often took the long road to the mall from the Annandale grounds and would stop for a while at the beautiful Viceregal Lodge (Rashtrapati Niwas) located on the picturesque observatory hill of Shimla. This architectural marvel is one of the most prominent historically significant sites in the region. I was so fascinated that I returned there several times in the next few years.

In 1948, Shiv Raj moved to Delhi and invited me to visit him. I took his bike and visited historical places like the Qutub Minar, Red Fort, Jama Masjid, the

Parliament House, and many more. He kindly invited me to visit him on a yearly basis.

In 1954, when I came to Glasgow, Scotland, I toured many lakes and islands within an eighty-mile radius. In the following years, I made time to tour greater Scotland and had the chance to visit historical places all over London.

In 1970, during my first visit to America, I had the opportunity to go to Niagara Falls and New York City, where I found humongous historical buildings like the United Nations headquarters, the Empire State Building, and the Statue of Liberty, which were quite fascinating. I toured so many new places and managed to see Mammoth Cave in Kentucky, the second-largest cave in the world, and I felt exhilarated, as though the whole world was within my reach.

In America, I've visited the following twelve most fascinating parks, the wonders and treasures of America.

> 2005—Wyoming
> Grand Teton National Park; Yellowstone National Park, home of geysers that shoot boiling water high into the air, mudholes that bubble like boiling soap, and waterfalls that thunder down spectacular canyons

> 2006—Utah
> Arches National Park; Canyon Land National Park; Bryce Canyon National Park, a geological splendor, the formation of heavenly temples by erosion of limestone; and Zion National Park, the

most beautiful national park, with multicolored peaks and cliffs rising above narrow canyons, a dramatic landscape whose visual aspects change with the sunlight throughout the day

2008—Arizona
Grand Canyon National Park, the legend, the sublime spectacle of nature, the gigantic hole in the ground, the result of millions of years of rock erosion; California: Yosemite National Park, Sequoia National Park. Yosemite is renowned for its spectacular waterfalls and rock formations as well as what is believed to be the largest and longest-living tree in the world at about 2,700 years old

2008—Las Vegas, Nevada; Hoover Dam, Grand Canyon, Arizona; CN Tower, Toronto; Niagara Falls, Canada

2011—Florida
Everglades National Park

2012—Calgary, Canada; Montana
Glacier National Park

I've also enjoyed global travels. In 2007, I traveled to the UK, France, Switzerland, Germany, the Netherlands, and Belgium, then back to London, and saw all the places of interest including the London Eye, wax museum, Eiffel Tower, Notre Dame, and Lake Lucerne. In 2008, I made a trip to the Valley of Kashmir for ten days by road from Jammu and visited all the important places, like Srinagar and its famous Mughal Gardens, Dal Lake, Gulmarg, Sonamarg, and Pahalgam.

Propelled by the spirit of an adventurer, I've voyaged from a tiny village in Punjab to the faraway corners of the world through many beautiful countries. I've seen serene lakes and towering peaks. I've seen everything.

In 2009, when I was in India, I was fortunate to visit Elephant Cave in Bombay, Ajanta Caves near Aurangabad, Ellora Caves near Aurangabad, and Khajuraho temples in Madhya Pradesh. I traveled from Delhi to Jaipur, back to Agra and Fatehpur Sikri, and down to Mathura. I visited Amritsar (Golden Temple), Jallianwala Bagh, and Wagah Border.

In September 2013, I made a trip from Ludhiana to Chandigarh to Bombay followed by Goa, Bangalore, Mysuru, Chennai, and Kerala State, making seven stops including Ooty and Kenya Kumari. My 2013 Indian adventure included a trip to Banaras and Nepal. There I saw the great Mount Everest and flew close to the top in an airplane. I even visited other places of interest like Kathmandu, Pokhara, and Chitwan in Nepal.

I still have a burning desire to see South American countries and even Hawaii. By the grace of God, I've achieved everything I ever wished for since my childhood. I am totally satisfied with my life. Thanks be to God. Thank you, America, and I love you.

Top: Zion National Park, Utah, USA
Middle Left: Sequoia National Park, California - Worlds largest and oldest living tree (2011)
Middle Right: Kollam, Karela, India
Bottom Left: Taj Mahal, India
Bottom Right: Ajanta Caves, near Aurangabad, India

CHAPTER THREE

PARENTAGE & BIRTH
1931

My parents and grandparents lived in a remote rural village called Bhullar in Punjab, an area of northwest India. My grandfather and his two brothers had connections with the local shoemakers and ran a couple of small shoe shops in the neighboring villages. They traveled by dirt road on camels to distribute their goods to shops, peasants, and others in distant villages. My grandfather's parentage is unknown to me.

My grandfather Gulab Chand and his four brothers died in middle age due to lack of medical care. Gulab Chand had two sons and two daughters. My father Amar Chand, the oldest of the four, was only twenty-five years of age and his younger brother Lekh Chand was only sixteen at the time of their father's death. The children had no education because of the rigid caste system and the grip of high-caste Brahmans over the lower castes was very strong.

In those days, at the beginning of the nineteenth century and before, there was no work in remote villages except farm work. Most poor villagers worked for Sikh or Muslim farmers for a handful of wheat or couple of chapatis at the end of the day. Some were weavers who made rough cloth for their fellow villagers. There was terrible poverty and misery and the future was very dim for many villagers.

My grandmother Bhani wanted my father to do some work of his own as my grandfather had left her some money to provide for the family. She was willing to support the family and use the money for their benefit. My father didn't know any profession except manual labor. His friends in other villages were doing leather tanning work and they promised to teach him, so my father opted for that profession. After spending a year with his friends in a faraway village, he started his own tanning work in a small way. He had to work very hard, looking for raw materials, tanning materials and then processing and selling it for a profit. My uncle was growing up and he started helping my father. His sisters also helped by fetching water from the well and doing light jobs. All the members of the family worked hard. My father attempted to get ahead in the business and pushed himself to make a decent living for his family.

In the meantime, his two cousins Lalu Ram and Dev Ram were growing up. They were older than my father. They were exercising a lot and growing stronger. They had a very hard time growing up under oppression and subjection to the local Jat farmers and other neighbors. In the culmination of a series of injustices over the years, they were pushed around a lot after their father died, when they were still young and innocent. Because of this, they developed a lust for revenge and became rebellious. They started beating up neighbors who were cruel to them. Sometimes they would cut the crops of the Jat farmers in the dark of night; other times they would hide the farmer animals in the sugar cane fields, then milk the cows and goats and drink all the milk or let them loose to feed on standing crops.

My father did not like this at all. Animosity against other people was brewing and chilling prospects emerged. My father had a difficult time running his business because of transportation. He took this opportunity to buy a few acres of arid land near the train station in Nakodar, seven miles from his village. He cleared the land of its plentiful wild bushes, dug a well there, and built a small house. Soon his cousins followed. People from other villages also bought land and settled in that area. A few years later, my father established a small leather-making business.

I was only one year old when my entire family moved to Nakodar in 1932. I was born on April 20, 1931, in the small, remote village of Bhullar in Punjab in the northwest of undivided India. I was the only young child in the house, and I remember that my sisters used to fetch me from the playing field and gave me a bath. My uncle Lekh Chand was very fond of me and took great care of me, especially since he had no children. Up to five years of age, I was a well- protected, spoiled child. My family never let me go far from them and I was well looked after by my sisters and uncle. We were all living as a family together under one roof that sheltered cousins and other close relatives. I have very faint memories of my uncle making me sit on a white horse. I'm unsure whether the horse belonged to my family or not. I must have been two or three years old then. I remember running on dirt roads after bullock carts and trying to jump on them for a ride. Often, I got hurt doing this.

Life was very tough after we moved to the new

place, as it was not an easy adjustment with easy answers. My father had a commanding personality and he inspired more and more people to move near the town for work and a better quality of life. There was a tremendous feeling of relief there, of throwing off the great burden of the higher castes and a new spirit of freedom to mind our business.

MY DEAR MOTHER

The outstanding impression my mother Raj Kaur left on my memory was due to her deep love for me and her generosity for others. She always tried to feed me well as she was worried about my health. She was a very simple though uneducated person. She was deeply religious, and every first day of the month (*Sangrand*), she would gather the young children, especially the girls, to feed them sweet rice and other treats of her choice. This was good charity, but sometimes she asked me to accompany her to a bush with a lot of holes where a big snake was supposed to live, and she would say a prayer. It was a very orthodox practice, and I was afraid of snakes and didn't enjoy it. Occasionally she used to go to the neighbors' or workers' houses to have a chat with them and find out how they were doing. I remember her ordering me to deliver a bag of wheat to a house for free. She lived a very simple life, not caring too much for anything. She was incredibly kind and generous and if she had any money, she gave it to the poor. She fasted every now and then and living on one meal a day was a habit for her. She was an easy-going person.

My mother had a strong sense of responsibility. I remember her missing the train because she was more worried about the cows than the train. She would shout at my sisters again and again to feed the cows and the dog. She loved walking and often visited relatives and friends on foot. Walking ten to twelve miles was relatively easy for her. She was very respectful to my father and her elders and never interfered in their affairs or argued, instead trusting them to be right all the time.

As I was the only young boy in the family, I was naturally my grandmother Bhani's favorite grandson. She was an old lady with a tremendous will of her own and was not accustomed to being ignored. She was a dominant old woman. When we were alone in the house, she used to sit with a stick in front of the main passage of the house in case I went out with some wheat to buy sweets from the Muslim lady vendor who used to come to our village. Then, I was an unyielding adversary with granite stubbornness toward my grandmother. She was very much against giving wheat away, but she didn't mind buying things with cash. She was well respected by my father and others, and I was very scared of her. She was a woman of principle and I learned a lot by being around her that served me well in the future.

MY FATHER

My father Amar Chand was a very simple person. He wore a turban, waistcoat, dhoti (loincloth), and gold earrings all his life. He had a fair complexion with a drooping mustache and a bald patch on his head. My father was a self-made person and had a lot of guts. He had no education as he was not allowed to go to school because of intense caste prejudice. He learned Punjabi (Gurmukhi) by his own efforts, including simple reading and writing and how to keep his accounts.

I liked and admired my father tremendously for his wisdom and extraordinary qualities, but I feared him, too. I didn't see him much during my early years as he was always busy working or helping people. He believed that if you don't help your neighbors or other needy people, there's no use living. He was a God-fearing person with strong convictions and a lot of religious beliefs. He was very sensible and confident but did not go to any Gurdwara or Mandir because of segregation and humiliation problems. He bought all the religious holy books, like the *Ramayana*, Mahabharata, *Guru Nanak Dev ki Sakhi*, and Guru Ravidass Deep, read them time and time again, and liked to hold discussions about religious matters late at night with a holy sadhu (holy person). He was the tallest in the family and his physical appearance in the house commanded attention. He was a superb specimen of humanity. He always respected his elders and others. My father was a lover of his clan and natural leader of the villagers. He was generous, loyal, and forbearing, a man of real integrity and deeply committed to moral and ethical principles. Therefore, he wielded great influence and respect in the community.

He grew up in an atmosphere of continual oppression and subjection of every kind. He had endured insults and humiliation by upper-caste Brahman Hindus, Jat Sikhs, and Muslims, and I noticed that he was very fearful of high-caste people. In order to survive, he left the old village and founded the new one near the train station and town in 1929. He inspired the people of his clan to move to the new village where they could earn their living. He helped many people and lifted the yoke of slavery from their shoulders.

He manifested sincerity and earnestness and his

winning personality endeared him to the public. Their reverence for my father was visible every moment. He was the most influential person in our village and the surrounding community. People used to come to him from far and near for advice and help. He was a pillar of wisdom and always courageously confronted evil with the power of love and respect. In his lifetime, he did his best to liberate the poor of his community from their shackles, and for this reason, people worshiped the ground my father walked on. He set a noble example that I didn't mind following. I still feel the effects of the noble morals and ethical ideals that I grew up with. They have been precious to me. My father instilled the same courage and manhood in me.

My father was a legend of hospitality. He loved to entertain strangers, sadhus (holy men), and passersby. He brought in wandering sadhus, fed them their choice of food, and later discussed religious matters with them. Long distance travelers always stopped at my father's workplace for rest and a smoke. He dearly loved his children and grandchildren.

He was very practical and a great organizer with a big heart. Two of his cousins, Blasa Rai and Ruldu Rai, moved to Harappa, now in Pakistan, to work for a prominent farmer for many years. Both were carrying debt and the interest was piling up. They were afraid to come back in case the lender acted. After years of hard work, my father managed to expand his business. He discussed the debt with his close friend, the elite Mohat Ram, a Brahman that he was willing to pay the principal his cousins had borrowed. Otherwise, the lender would keep pursuing them and wasting his time. Under pressure from Mohat Ram and other leaders, the lender agreed to settle the debt without interest. After clearing the debt, my father brought his cousins back with their children and belongings and employed them in his workplace. The children were of marriageable age and my father organized and arranged marriages for five girls in only a few months. Big tents were pitched in the huge backyard of my house and the necessary items for the marriages were purchased. I was given the great responsibility of looking after the guests, and I recall the event clearly even today.

The death of my father's beloved younger brother Lakh Chand, who died young in 1941, was a terrible blow to him. For a long time, he sat still without a word, laden with grief. It was a cruel blow to him. His closest and dearest comrade was suddenly gone and the burden of looking after the family fell on him.

He sacrificed a lot to raise his younger brother's children after his death and gave half of his property to them. But these spoiled and selfish children never appreciated what he did for them. He even passed on the task of looking after his brother's children and grandchildren to me, so extreme was his love for his brother and his family. When he was young, my father worked so hard day and night to raise his youngest brother and two sisters and to help others that he became sick. He suffered from chronic disease, and later in his life, he had to do away with a lot of things. My mother or sisters cooked separate meals for him without chilies and masala. He was well looked after by his family; otherwise, he wouldn't have survived for long. My father was very kind and compassionate. Whenever his poor nieces, cousins, and other family came to visit him, he always paid their fare for the train or tonga (horse cart). Some of the poorest begged him for work because they were in debt, and my father always responded positively and helped them settle their debts.

Once a booking agent disappeared with a large sum of money. My father found the sub agent he had given the money to and demanded it back, but the agent refused. My father reported him to the police, and the police captured him and started beating him in front of my father. My father soon walked away from the scene and came home. He narrated the entire event to my mother with eyes full of tears. My mother also became emotional when she saw my father's condition and told me to go to the police station, take the report back, and free the sub agent from jail.

My father never renounced his deep-rooted sense of inferiority and his docile acceptance of the law of fate. He was obsessed with the feeling of inferiority and inadequacy, which troubled me greatly throughout the years I spent with him. He always greeted those he called high-caste Brahmans, Bunias, and Jat Sikhs by standing with folded hands and not getting any sincere response in return. I think fear rooted in his feeling of inferiority deprived him of the moral courage to stand against evil and defend his rights. He had adjusted to the insults and segregation after so many years of oppression and subjection. Although this injustice always pained him, he was unable to stand against it due to his lack of education and misguided beliefs in destiny. I didn't want my father to bow with folded hands before the wrong people. It was hurting me when they were not responding at all. I think it reduced our dignity and stature. But he couldn't help it as he and millions of others were sucked into a rotten system by the coercion of the upper castes. Perhaps this was the only way to live peacefully among tyrants, bigots, and troublemakers in the nineteenth century and before. From a self-made businessman to a passionate community helper, he had pursued his big dreams of building a better life for his family and community. He was a survivor. My father died, but his memory remains with me as a dear and precious possession.

UNCLE LEKH CHAND

My uncle was very fond of me and I was the only child in the household at that time. He was younger than my father and their two sisters. Like the others, he never went to school because of the tense caste prejudice and instead began helping my father at a very young age. He was deeply loved by my father and his mother and turned out to be a hardworking and responsible person. When my father fell sick, he took full responsibility for their work along with my elder brother Shenker Dutt. When our family moved to Nakodar, it was extremely challenging to establish the business in a new place and my uncle and brother worked day and night to succeed. Uncle Lekh looked after my elder brother and fed him well so he remained healthy and strong. He resented it greatly when my father offered to help. and he asked him to sit next to him and supervise the work. He also resented it when my father had to look for help in a local town to write a letter to his customers in Lahore or Kasur. Perhaps this was reason why he was so anxious to put me through school. I believe my uncle contributed a lot toward the family's welfare and helped my father when we moved from the old village and we were poor. My good father never ignored or forgot his dear brother's contribution till the last day of his life.

I only remember my uncle and my older sisters from

when I was two to three years old. I recall him taking me to school with my two distant cousins and enrolling us. I always complained to him, not my father, when I was in trouble in school or if I wanted something from a shop. Uncle Lekh took me with him whenever he went to see his relatives and always bought new clothes for me. I was his pet.

He was a very humble and kind person and always asked my father to help his cousins or others whenever they were in trouble. It was my uncle who forced my father to bring his cousins, Blasa Rai and Ruldu Rai, and their families back from Harappa (Pakistan) and give them work. He was very religious, like my father, and asked my father to build a spare room for prayers, etc. Unfortunately, he died very young, at the age of thirty-nine. I, my mother, my uncle, and his son had contracted smallpox. The rest of us recovered after two months, but my uncle passed away because of the seriousness of his illness. The whole family was in shock. It was a terrible blow and my father was in a lot of pain. It was sudden and catastrophic. Before dying, my uncle told my father that he had full confidence and trust in him to look after his two sons better than he could. And so, my father did, but I think he spoiled them because they did not learn anything and became useless and later turned against him. Like them, their children became backstabbers. I suffered a lot at their hands, and they never appreciated my or my father's help. Instead they became formidable adversaries.

My mother and my daughter Kamlesh (1954)

CHAPTER FOUR

CHILDHOOD & YOUTH

My childhood was not a happy one like that of a normal child. It was bleak and atrocious. In India, the 1930s and the prior period were like a manmade madhouse on earth. I'll never forget my first day in primary school and the rest of the days I spent there. There was not a day when I didn't feel insulted and humiliated. It was April of 1936 and I was five years old, a young, innocent village child who knew nothing about the city and the outside world. It wasn't my fault where I was born and what sort of work my parents were doing. And despite that, the school system was so bad that the teachers could do anything they wanted just because a student came from a low caste. They were paid by the government to look after and teach children, but it was the opposite experience for my family and me.

My distant cousins had to clean the teachers' shoes and were often forced to sweep the floor. The teachers were tyrants. They were fundamentalists. They had a splinter of contempt embedded in their minds. They were a generation of unthinking segregationists, and altering their mindset was impossible. It's difficult to conceal my emotions now, even after eighty-three years. I hesitate to use the words that most accurately convey their behavior. I always dreaded teachers' authority and actions.

Up to the age of five, before starting school in 1936, my childhood was sheltered by my big sisters and uncle Lekh Chand. I enjoyed constant attention from a large and loving family. I could do anything and get away with it. I was a spoiled child. My wrongs were covered by my uncle, who was very fond of me. The only person in the household I was afraid of was my father. He was always busy with work and I hardly saw him when I was young. My uncle, on the other hand, was very anxious and enthusiastic to send me to primary school. He took me and my two distant cousins, Sardar Ram and Shenker Rai, both older than me, to the District Board Primary School situated in the heart of the town of Nakodar, next to an old *tehsil* building (county building) on high ground, about two miles from my home. He enrolled the three of us and gave all the information to the teachers about our age and caste. Our religion was recorded as Hindu and our caste was chamar, considered a low but meticulous and productive class.

ILL-TREATMENT BY TEACHERS

The next day, my sister dressed me in new clothes, and I went to school along with my cousins. There were no benches or desks, and the children sat on long mats. In our class, the teacher told us to sit in the back of row on the bare floor, a few feet away from the other students. I used to refuse and tell the teacher that my good clothes would get dirty. He would shout at me in anger: "You are untouchable, son of a leather-worker, and you are not allowed to mix with other, high-caste boys!" His words hit me like a bullet. The teacher's cruel remarks perturbed me enough to keep me awake that night. He forced me and my cousins to sit uncomfortably on the bare floor, knees raised, a few feet away from the high-caste boys on their long mats. That was the first time someone ever shouted at me, snatched my smile, and I learned that I belonged to a low caste. I had to swallow all the insults, and I was in tears, filled with anger, but couldn't do anything. I wanted to run away from school, but that was impossible. I felt infinitely awkward. My distant cousins and I were segregated and mistreated. That was the warm welcome the teacher and other students gave us on the first day of school. My enthusiasm to attend school and learn was shattered. I sobbed all the way home. I didn't speak to anyone all evening; I was very depressed. Nothing could bring a smile to my face. To this day, it's still so vivid in my mind.

The following day I refused to go to school, but my uncle insisted and soothed me. He took me by the hand and walked me to school. He pleaded with the teacher, with folded hands, to treat me nicely. My teacher was Gulani Mohammed, a well-built Muslim man with a fancy turban, baggy trousers, and a long shirt. He was the Urdu language teacher. He didn't like me even though I paid close attention to the lessons. I used to get into a lot of trouble with my father for cursing the teacher in his presence. My father often told me that the teacher was my guru and I must respect him no matter what.

In second grade, my teacher's name was Nand Lal. He must've been Hindu, Jain, or Brahman. He was not as rude, and more soft-spoken. He dressed in pajamas (wide pants) and a tunic and topi (cap). Above all, he was also a callous brute. Whether these old teachers were Muslim, Hindu, Jain, or Sikh, they all put religious interests above the welfare of their poor and low-caste students. They were all racist, cruel, and obstinate. They all adhered to one principle: that we were working-class people, untouchables, the scum of the earth. We weren't good enough and must be kept away and discouraged from school and learning. They were possessed by a religious devil. This was an endless age of woe and suffering. Because of this unflinching suffering and humiliation in schools, a lot of poor and downgraded people didn't like to send their children to school. For me, these were dreary and difficult hours spent in a hostile environment.

SCHOOL FAILURE

There were three boys from my community and village, Ram Nath, Fathe Chand, and Deen Ram, who were three years ahead of me. My distant cousins and I jumped ahead to second grade and they all failed fourth grade. The headmaster used to announce the results of those who passed and failed after the morning prayer. I remember that Ram Nath and Deen Ram were in tears and Fathe Chand was soothing them, saying it was good that they had all failed and wouldn't have to suffer more degradation and humiliation. They didn't have to come to school anymore. That was the end of their education and schooling.

My distant cousin Shenker Rai left school after passing second grade and his family moved to District Montgomery (now in Pakistan) to do peasant work for a well-known farmer. I was left in class with only one companion, Sardar Ram. A lot of anger developed between us and sometimes we fought on the dirt road leading home until blood flowed from our mouths and heads. Sometimes passersby had to separate us. I tried not to tell my parents about the fights or my wounds and scratches, but Sardar Ram complained bitterly to his parents. His mother used to come to my house with complaints. My father always took their side and often reprimanded me, warning me to keep out of trouble. His advice stood me in good stead in the later years of my life. However, Sardar Ram discontinued his studies after passing primary school and started helping his father with the farm work.

THE START OF LETTER WRITING

In school, I was a devoted student who never missed a day of class. I was good at my studies. My uncle made sure that I reviewed my studies at home and did my homework. My handwriting was very good, and my older brother Shenker Dutt, who didn't finish fourth grade, used to tell my father that I could write very well. One Sunday morning, my father instructed me to go to our workplace with my reed pen and my little earthen inkpot. I stood wonderstruck. I was surprised and inquisitive as to what he wanted out of me with my pen and ink. He told me to sit beside my elder brother, who was sitting on the wet floor and working. I didn't like this, but it was a strict order from my father. He told me to put two dry bricks next to my brother and sit on them. Then my uncle handed me a postcard and my brother Shenker Dutt dictated the address of a leather merchant in Lahore, now in Pakistan, named Haji Mohammed Wakit Mohammed Ismal Leather Merchants. He directed me to write a message on the reverse as my father stated. Then they asked me to read the letter back to them. My uncle Lekh Chand immediately took the letter to post it at the train station about half a mile away. This was the beginning of my letter writing to customers and relatives, just after I passed the third grade of primary school in 1939. After fifteen days, the answer to the letter arrived in Urdu and my brother read it to my father. My uncle Lekh Chand was so exhilarated that he distributed sweets to the whole village. My letter writing and education made a lasting impact on our society. My father soon found another customer, Mohammed Ali Mohammed Isman Leather merchants in Kasur (now in Pakistan), and started communicating and visiting them.

They were very proud and happy, but I wasn't. The letter writing was extra work for me on top of my schoolwork and I hardly had time to play. Every day I came home from school, tired and exhausted after walking two miles in the burning heat of the sun, and there was always somebody waiting for me to read or write a letter to their relatives. I couldn't just refuse them for fear of my father, because he believed in helping villagers and neighbors. My writing was a big milestone for my father and uncle, and they were very proud of me. But they soon forgot and took for granted that it represented progress for their business.

After tireless effort, my uneducated father succeeded in communicating for business purposes. As the saying goes, every thousand-mile journey begins with a first step, and letter writing was the first step toward progress. It opened a channel of communication, something my father needed urgently. Before this, my father used to go to town and pay someone to write letters. More than anything else, he resented disclosing his business deals to other people and wasted a lot of time traveling to town in the scorching heat. My letter writing gave him a lot of comfort. It inspired optimism, giving him the feeling that the impassable barriers that had always confronted him were doomed. He started respecting me and looking after me. Now he was taking care of me and I became an indispensable assistant to him. I became well known throughout the village as an educated boy.

HOBBIES

I didn't have any friends in school, and I was isolated and neglected. But in my village, I was a friend to everybody. I used to play revolving top (*lattu*) with an ailing boy named Bansi Lal, son of my uncle Lalu Ram. He was born disabled and couldn't move much, but I really liked him. I used to spend time with him in his house until he passed away. A year or two later, I started playing Gilli Danda, an ancient sport of the Indian subcontinent, with village boys and was very good at it. Gilli Danda consists of striking a short, sharpened wooden peg with a long stick. The peg bounces up from the ground, and then the player hits it in midair. During the winter months, I used to go outside as soon as the morning sun was up and meet my friends, basking in the sunshine and gossiping or playing marbles around a hole in the ground in the backyard of my house. Often my father called me in the middle of the game to tend to him or his visitors with fresh hookah (tobacco and water pipe). Our house was always full of people visiting from the neighborhood. Hookah smoking was very common in villages and maintaining hookah with fresh water and fresh tobacco was my responsibility. Giving fresh hookah to a visitor was considered the best treat in those days. My brother often smoked Red Lamp cigarettes, a popular and cheap brand back then.

Besides playing these small games, I loved to see dramas. There were a couple of popular drama groups from town called Mulsian and Chabbewal. These drama teams were contracted by different villages on special occasions. Dramas were performed at night. Surrounding villages were alerted to the presence of drama parties by the beating of drums. My father didn't like me to go anywhere, so when he was asleep, I used to go out with my friends at nighttime and travel two to three miles on foot, then come back home before he woke up. I did this many times; it was great fun.

Another popular game was wrestling. Tournaments were held in different villages at different times. For me, the nearest villages were Solaan about one mile from my house. There were several good wrestlers from different towns and villages. I remember one named Gurudar, from Shankar. He was very popular in those days. I used to wrestle with boys my own age, sometimes at night, just for fun or exercise. I had many other interests and passions when I was young, and these formed the basis of my successes or failures in life.

Another favorite pastime was bathing in the rain. During monsoon weather, I was always outside in the big front or backyard of the house, digging to sow seeds for kikar trees. Other times, I would buy orange and banana trees from a nursery out of my pocket money and lie to my father that a friend gave them to me for free because he thought it was a waste of money.

I had a habit of disappearing from the house without warning and my sister often found me climbing a kikar tree, peeling the resinous material from its branches to make ink for schoolwork, or hiding behind berry bushes. I was very fond of small berries. There were a lot of wild berry bushes along the railroad track, and I used to spend a lot of time and energy plucking the ripe and delicious berries from among the sharp thorns. Most of the time the thorns pierced my hands, but I still enjoyed eating those fresh berries and soon forgot all about the thorns. I enjoyed a very carefree life in my small village when I was young.

I never flew any kites, but I loved to watch. Two boys from my neighborhood were very good at kite flying. One day I joined them and wanted to learn how to do it. On one occasion, while we were flying our kite on the flat rooftop of my big house, leaning back and forth, pulling the string and then loosening it, we became so engrossed that we forgot we were on the roof. I fell ten to twelve feet onto an upside-down stack of logs and hurt my head badly. My father burned some old cloth, put the charred scraps on the wound to stop the bleeding, and took me to the hospital. I have that big scar on my head today and it reminds me of my lesson in kite flying.

I developed a nasty habit when I was in primary school. I loved fresh sugarcane. I used to follow farmers' bullock carts loaded with sugarcane. Sometimes the bundles became loose and some sugarcane fell on the ground. I picked up the fallen sugarcane and ate it. Other times I stole it from the bundle to quench my thirst for sugarcane. My father didn't like my habit and often reprimanded me. Later he started buying sugarcane that wasn't harvested in the fields from farmers. Soon I became friends with the farmers' sons, Babu Singh and Lakha Singh, and they gave me a higher quality sugarcane (*ganna*) that I appreciated very much. The best was *desi ganna*. It had a very nice flavor. I miss it and wish I could find it here in the US.

AN ONWARD JOURNEY

My elder brother Shenker Dutt was a hardworking person and during his leisure time, he loved reading romance novels and playing cards. He used to buy small books, and later, in fourth and fifth grade, I started reading the ones that he kept at work. I read *Heer Ranjha, Sassi Punnu Sohnii Mahiwal, Dulla Bhatti,* and others at the age of ten or eleven. I became a very fluent reader of the Urdu language. At times I tried to help my brother and uncle in leather-making, but I often cut my hands with the sharp tools or fell into a deep pit full of tanning material.

Besides playing games, I did a lot of daily chores, helping my mother and sisters cut grass, cook, wash, and fetch water. Even at an early age, I was not afraid to do anything and remained faithful to the family. My father made me responsible for buying vegetables and other foodstuffs from the market and looking after the house and relatives at a young age. So, in my teens I was more a message boy for the large family than an industrious student. The older family members worked very hard in the 1930s to make a living and I also did my best to support them.

CHAPTER FIVE

PRIMARY SCHOOL 1936

My primary school, the district board primary school, was situated in the heart of town, next to an old *tehsil* (county building) on higher ground than the town's streets. I spent four years at this boys' school in Nakodar. The school building was very old and made of small bricks. All the rooms were a good size, and in the center of the school, there was a big peepal tree surrounded by a stupendous open lot and schoolrooms, where the morning prayers were held. From grade one to grade four, high-caste students used to sit on long mats made of jute. There were no benches or chairs in the classrooms except for the teacher.

Caste prejudice and segregation were very intense then, and the low-caste students were prohibited from mixing with other students. The teacher told them to sit at the end of the row, on the bare floor. There were no notebooks or fancy pens and I used a homemade pen made from a wild reed. To write on, I used a *phattie* (a rectangular piece of wood). I used to make my own black ink, and in an emergency, I went to the bookshop called Ganga Rai Fatam Chand in Bansawala Bazaar. This was an established shop and I bought all my books there. I covered my books with a piece of cloth and most of the time I carried them on my head.

Near the school, in the center of the town, there were fruit and sweets shops. I was not allowed to touch the fruit or sweets and had to tell the shopkeeper from a distance what I wanted by pointing a finger. Some shopkeepers were rude and always robbed children, so I made a point to go to the shopkeepers who were kinder and more honest with me. The biggest problem was drinking water. The school had a peon; he was a high-caste person. I used to go to him and ask for drinking water. He poured water from his pitcher or a big pot into my hands as I cupped them around my mouth, but most of the time the water hit my forehead and my nose before my mouth. I used to get my clothes wet every time. The curse of being an untouchable was at its worst in those days, and as a helpless and innocent child, I suffered a lot.

Flogging of children was quite common, and children were punished for coming late to school, leaving school without permission, and not doing homework. Sometimes harsh punishment was applied to children by making them sit like a ball for a long time. There was one incident that occurred in third grade, when my cousin Sardar Ram and I were very late to school because of the heavy rain. Halfway there, we made up our minds to skip school and ended up at the local train station, where farmers sold sugarcane. It was then loaded on railroad wagons to take to sugar mills. We loved sugarcane and went roaming about to steal some. We were picked up by distant cousin's father. He brought me home to my father, who wanted to know why I'd deceived him. My excuse about the rain wasn't good enough, and he beat me. I ran around the village to hide from my father. The next day in class, my teacher hit my hand many times with a stick as punishment for being absent without permission and I grew blisters.

In those days, there were no houses or trees between my village Nai-Abadi and the town of Nakodar . It was a desolate stretch of one and a half miles, and one could see the golden domes of Ram Temple in town from the roof of my house. The footpath to Nakodar was sandy, with cactus bushes and wild reed bushes here and there along its edges. Sometimes I found wild watermelon vines and another vine called Tumee, (Punjabi slang), growing here and there near the sandy path. These naturally grown delicate watermelons were very fascinating and pleasing to me, and I often spent time in the cool morning looking for and sometimes hiding baby watermelons. My classmate Sardar Ram had a habit of stealing and annoying me. He always pulled my watermelons out of hiding and destroyed them. So, even about small matters like melons, we used to fight bloody battles with each other.

I used to wear a turban and gold earrings. My turban stayed with me until the end of primary school. There were rumors of kidnappings of young children. Some evil men were selling children to Brahman priests to be sacrificed to please their gods. So, my parents took the gold earrings off my ears on the advice of my teacher and made me go to school with groups or follow the group of men.

Caste prejudice was very bad in those days and we had a lot of trouble with drinking water. Cold water was not readily available and sometimes we looked for a place to quench our thirst. I can well recollect those days. The teachers weren't interested in us. Boys of high caste were not willing to touch us or associate with us. The school day used to end at about 2:00 p.m. and I had to walk two miles in the scorching sun. Sometimes I forgot my shoes at home and had to walk barefoot in the afternoon. Outside the town, near Ram Mandir, there was a big banyan tree with big green leaves. In the shadow of this tree that spread its dense foliage over the temple courtyard, I used to rest or play for a while and then collect the fallen leaves and tie them to my feet to save them from the burning sand. There was swamp and shallow ground in the vicinity of Ram Temple and in monsoon rainy season it was too tough to cross to go home and I often climbed rough hedged.

I hated going to primary school because of segregation and caste prejudice and I wept a lot almost every day whenever I was alone. I was insulted and abused by the teacher and students and I had no real friends. I felt depressed and sick and never gained weight. My mother used to worry a lot about me. My primary school years were the worst years of my life. Fear of punishment from my father and love from my uncle kept me going to school; otherwise, I would have stayed away from school like millions of others. Because of ill treatment in and outside school, I felt a lot of mental depression and became sick. My parents took me to the hakim (doctor), who treated me with all kinds of special herbs and juices, but nothing worked and I remained sick, losing weight until I went to college, where I finally felt free of discrimination and separation.

CHAPTER SIX

MY VILLAGE

The small village where I grew up, Nai-Abadi, is a suburb of Nakodar and about half a mile from the Nakodar Junction train station in the state of Punjab. Nakodar is connected by railroad to the cities of Ludhiana, Jalandhar, and Ferozepur. The railroad track to Jalandhar and Ludhiana passed only a few hundred yards from my home and sometimes the smoke clouds that the train engine spewed blinded my eyes. Villagers used to hear the rumbling thunder and whistle of the local train, and it served as a sort of clock for villagers in the 1930s.

The best thing my father did for the family was to move from his old village of Bhullar, a predominantly Jat Sikh (caste) village in a remote rural area, to Nakodar. By doing so, he got rid of the yoke of slavery imposed by Jat farmers and others and gained a little bit of freedom. In 1930, he established his house and business in Nakodar next to the train station, one and a quarter mile away. My father was a commanding personality who inspired his community members toward better and easier living near the town and helped his clan move to Nakodar. He was committed to making a difference in people's lives and so he did.

PROFESSIONAL WORK
In this small village, all the inhabitants were connected to the leather industry either directly or indirectly. My father Amar Chand and my distant uncle Lalu Ram worked their way up in the business. Others who made big strides were Mukhi Ram and Ratu Ram. These businesspeople worked hard and hired local people for help. Another man, Shuda Ram, came later from the village of Bath Kalan and established his leather business. Bath Kalan was connected to Nakodar by dirt roads through the villages of Maheyma and Aulak, then from Nai-Abadi to Nakodar.

In the 1930s, my small village was surrounded by arable land and pasturage for miles on three sides, and the other side was the train station only half a mile away. There were three wells in the village fitted with leather or steel buckets to bring the water up. The village had a lot of trees and greenery, including one big garden containing fruit trees and flowers established by Dharma Ram, son of Ratu Ram.

My father had a big house containing seven rooms and a veranda where the whole family was accommodated. We always had two cows for milk, butter, and yogurt. A big room was built separately to accommodate the cows during winter nights. The back wall of my house, which faced the agriculture fields, must have been seventy feet long and made of solid red bricks. The front walls were also all solid brick. The walls separating the rooms were mud brick. My father also had a few empty plots in the village.

LACK OF UTILITIES

There was no electricity in those days, and we used kerosene lamps and oil candles for light at night. The village didn't have a drainage system, so the dirty rainwater collected in the low land. We had no toilets, so all the villagers relieved themselves far away, in the fields filled with crops or behind big bushes. The only popular recreation for the villagers was hookah, and it was like an inseparable companion. My father had two hookahs. In the evening or during leisure time, my father and his cousins used to get together and sit in a circle with the hookah and indulge in all sorts of gossip. They discussed the latest market rates and other important family matters. Dussehra and Diwali were undoubtedly the big events of the year. Villagers attended these fairs in large numbers. I used to oversee buying things like *laddu*, *jalebi*, and *burfi* (desserts) for the house and candles for lighting and decorating the house, workplace, and even our ancestors' graves so we could ask for their blessings. My father used to send me to town to look for his cousin Charanji Ram, who was very poor but an addicted gambler who believed there was no Diwali without gambling. He used to lose all his money gambling instead of buying sweets for his children.

My father's aunt Rudda was nearly ninety years old and had weak eyesight. She lived alone in the house next to ours and my father used to send me to sleep over there to keep watch over her and help her if needed. Her sons and their families were living in Harappa in District Montgomery, now in Pakistan. In 1931, the average life expectancy was only 27 years. A lot of young children were dying due to malnutrition and cholera and lack of medical care. Every day or night, one could hear women and children wailing for their dead family members in the villages.

My father, my uncle Lekh Chand, and my big brother Shenker Dutt were the main working people in our household. Sometimes they hired local temporary help. My sisters and I used to help fetch water from the well. Leather manufacturing required a lot of water and it was a tough job to fill the pits with water every day. We had no pump because there was no electricity and other pumps were not economical.

My father was a very shrewd and sensible person. I remember a time when we would strip bark from Kikar trees and then dry and crush the bark with big hammers. Some years later, someone invented a crushing machine and we used to work very late at the crushing machine to get the tanning material ready for the next day. My father put everyone to work except my mother, who did household work and cooking at home. We did work very hard for ourselves, but we were happy because we had a sense of freedom and inner peace. The old feeling of oppression and frustration, when one Jat Sikh could intimidate the whole village and no one would venture from their home after sunset, was completely gone. Sometimes we worked till ten or eleven at night at the bark-crushing machine and then came home through the fields and on the dirt road, where we often encountered big snakes along the sandy path. We used to change our direction and leave the snakes alone.

A TURNING POINT

Moving to Nakodar from the old village was a big turning point in my life as I grew up free from the shadow of high-caste, racist Brahmans, Sikhs, and Muslims. I grew up in my community as a caste-free and carefree person, which had a big impact on my future life. My community members who lived in predominantly Jat Sikh, Hindu, or Muslim villages had a very hard time. They were looked down upon as inferior and treated like slaves. In these villages, men, women, and children were sucked into a system of untouchability and segregation, whereas in my village, we lived as free people and held our heads high without fear of backlash.

In Nai-Abadi, inhabitants were descendants of two different villages, Bhullar and Kila. The whole village was like a close-knit family, looking after each other and living side by side in great harmony. I remember my father playing cards, laughing and enjoying the game in the company of the Kila people. They helped each other find suitable matches for their children. They shared each other's joys and sorrows. In the middle of the 1930s, Ratu Ram, Mukhi Ram, and company bought five acres of land behind my house, leaving a twelve-foot-wide space for a dirt road. I played with my friends in this open space all the time. A few years later, Shuda Ram constructed a big two-story modern brick house, a big deal in those days as most of the village houses were made of mud bricks. At the same time, my father constructed a single room, twelve by twelve feet, right in the middle of our house to store expensive items and money for fear of thieves. My village's leather businessmen were more well off than most of the Hindus, Muslims, and Sikhs in the surrounding villages and some of them viewed us with contempt. Most of the inhabitants had only one or two cows for milk and yogurt and some of the village women used to cut the grass from the fields or pull weeds and grass from farmers' crops to feed their animals.

Some years later, Shuda Ram's younger brother Khem Chand from Bath Kalan bought a horse and cart for private purposes and used to ride around Nakodar and our village. This was a real luxury. He became popular because none of the other town dwellers had this kind of luxury.

Although most of the villagers were engaged in the leather industry, there were odd ones who did like to work for farmers. The village was economically better off than others, but we were still treated badly outside its boundaries. We had no barber, so we hired one from a village called Sidhwan to cut our hair and hired workers to do other jobs on special occasions. I remember going to the blacksmith in a village called Mahewan to sharpen our working and kitchen tools and purchase new ones. The same day we had an appointment with the carpenter who used to mend our broken wooden objects and make new ones for us, and then we had a few Muslim women vendors come to our village to sell vegetables and other items. These people didn't love our work, but they loved our money. We bought fodder (*sayngi*) from nearby fields and cut grass ourselves when needed for our cattle and buffalo.

The tiny village was very religious, but we didn't have a place of worship. So, my uncle Lekh Chand pressed my father to build a special room where he could keep holy books and the whole village could come and attend readings. In those days, we didn't have any qualified doctors in the town or village; instead, we had witch doctors. Thus, many children died due to lack of proper care. We had no primary school in the village. The only primary school was in the heart of the town, about two miles away. A lot of people didn't like to send their children to school because of the long distance, poverty, burning heat, mistreatment by teachers, and possibility of kidnapping. The high school was only a mile away, across the agricultural fields on Mahatpur Road. When I started writing letters after third grade, a lot of children started going to school, but they didn't finish primary or high school because of the problems I listed above.

There were no banks in the town except one Hindu cooperative bank, and we didn't like to go there because of discrimination. We hid our money in the ground or in a secret safe place. In my house, I oversaw the money when I was young and had to hide the keys for our safety. The village had no radio, gramophone, or telephone, and definitely not a television, which wasn't even invented yet. Nobody could read the newspaper, and its use wasn't prevalent.

We passed our time by playing various games, slumbering in the warmth of the afternoon sun, or looking after our cows. Nobody in the village had a clock or watch except Shuda Ram, who was fond of pocket watches and elegant clothes. We used to tell the time by the whistle of the train engine or the shadow of the house. The village had plenty of greenery and trees throughout. I was very fond of trees and my parents found me digging to plant trees in monsoon weather while everyone was inside cooking and eating sweet roti or other food and having fun. There was no bicycle in the whole village, and I was the first one in my family to learn how to ride a bicycle in 1944.

A lot of beggars came to our village. They always asked for grain or money, but never accepted food. I think even the Muslim beggars considered us low caste. They didn't like us as people, but they liked our grain and money. My mother was very generous and believed that the more you give to charity, the more you receive from God. My father was very religious, too. He was fond of sadhus, and if he saw someone on the road, he begged them to come to the village and accommodated their wishes. He believed sadhus were educated and wise and tried to learn from them about spiritual matters.

A BIG DISADVANTAGE

Besides the freedoms we enjoyed, we had one big disadvantage: We were making leather by very primitive methods. Since manufacturing was mostly a wet process involving greases, chemicals, and water, we didn't know how to take care of effluents properly, which caused a smell, especially during the hot, humid season. The orthodox Hindus, Muslims, and Sikhs made a big deal of it and became vigorous critics of our industry, often covering their noses when they passed by the village because they had never worked for their living and were born with silver spoons in their mouths. Some of my own community's people detested this industry because they would rather live in slavery to the Jat Sikhs or Hindus than in the freedom of their body and soul from oppression and subjection to evil. But we were opposed to it because we loved our social and economic freedom more than anything else. We had an inner feeling of satisfaction that we had preserved our self-respect and dignity. Our homes were comfortable, and we lived the way we wanted to and enjoyed the fellowship of a close-knit community.

For my brave and prudent father, this was a great achievement. Because we dealt in leather, the orthodox and illiterate called us chamar with hatred and contempt.

They were stupid, and to them, the word chamar didn't sit right in their throats. After all, what's wrong with it? They're ignorant because they've never done anything except high-class begging, cheating or looting. Because I was born into this profession and loved it, I became a chamar to the core (American untouchable) by studying leather sciences (Chemistry of proteins and natural and synthetic products) and spent a profitable life in leatherworking, enjoying dignity and comfort with my well-educated family, neighbors and friends.

THE BLACK SHEEP

In every village, besides good people, there's always a black sheep. My village had the same problem. Khem Chand, who was a resident of Bath Kalan, had a luxury cart and horse and became popular with bureaucrats and city dwellers. He had a dominant personality and thought of himself as the leader and spokesman for my village, which was wrong. To win favor for himself and keep the bureaucrats happy, he never spoke for the benefit of my villagers. His damnable motive was to keep my village down. He was full of jealousy and didn't like many villagers because they didn't bow before him. Many villagers didn't know what he was doing behind their backs and the house taxes increased every year for everyone, including very poor residents. Because the villagers were illiterate and afraid, they didn't bother to complain about the taxes. I was in ninth grade and used to read all the mail in Urdu for my father. He always complained about receiving tax notices, but never did anything although the letter instructed us to complain. Because he, like the others, was uneducated, he never went to town to see the tax department officer. This time I made a point to take my father to the tax officer on the date a meeting was held every year in the *tehsil* in Nakodar. Nobody knew us except some townspeople. We sat on a brick platform surrounding a peepal tree near the meeting of city representatives and tax officers. Every representative defended his area's people. We were surprised to see Nobit Ram of Nakodar Dana Mandi (grain market), who defended Devu Raj Charn Lal a Bania, the owner of the grocery shop, regarding the tax increase. This shopkeeper was a millionaire, but never wore shoes or a shirt while working in the shop. Nobit Ram said he lived like a beggar, had no income or clothes, and couldn't pay any taxes.

One chair was empty, and we saw Khem Chand reaching for it, but it was for the representative of my village. Now we learned who was behind the curtain, pulling the strings. He was a hidden genius committed to an ideology. The tax officer announced the representative of my village and Khem Chand said that he was present. The tax officer started questioning him, asking about the business of Ratu Ram. He simply said it was very good. Then the officer asked about Mukhi Ram. Khem Chand said his business was better than Ratu Ram's and that Lalu Ram's business was doing better than both. The tax officer asked him about my father Amar Chand. Khem Chand said his business was very good and he was doing better than all three of them. His remarks made me very angry and I wondered how he knew about our business. He didn't know what he was talking about.

Simultaneously I exclaimed that he was our accountant and knew all about our business. Our taxes were raised fifty rupees over the previous year and the poor people's taxes were also raised a half rupee. This was Khem Chand's doing behind our backs because the people were illiterate. I filed a case in court against the tax officer and our taxes were reduced significantly. Khem Chand met my father and I in a bazaar and my father pleaded with him not to harm the poor village people. Acrimoniously, he accused me of insulting him in front of the tax officer and his friends. My father said to him, "You're rich, and I'm rich. Why don't you and I pay all the taxes for everybody in the village and keep the poor people free of taxes?" He clamored that I was comparing him with Devu Raj Charn Lal a Bania (the Hindu grocer) who never wore a shirt or shoes. The same Bania (in my presence) had offered his brother Shuda Ram a price for him and his family, his house, and everything else because Shuda Ram insulted him when Devu Raj approached him to buy manure for his agricultural fields. Without listening too much, he walked away.

People lived peacefully side by side in the village. They needed harmony, not discord. Khem Chand drove a wedge between the villagers. He succeeded in widening the gulf and poisoning relationships. Civil suits were fought, but he never let any agreement take shape. After a few years of running back and forth to the local court, my father won the case and Khem Chand stopped causing trouble for the villagers. Although he was very popular among the townspeople, many in my village despised him for his haughtiness and bossiness. He was quite different from Shuda Ram, Dunni Ram, and his other brothers.

The other black sheep was Ram Pal, the youngest son of Mukhi Ram. He had good looks and was the most well-dressed boy in the village and school. He was very spoiled. Like everyone else, he was married at an early age, when he was in tenth grade. After two days of marriage, he battered his innocent wife for no reason, then insulted his in-laws and put them out of the house during the night. He was my classmate for a year, and I tried to keep away from him. He used to keep a knife with him all the time and used it on one of his own cousins, Prem Chand, son of Ratu Ram. At our high school, some Brahman students cursed us. He got his knife out and luckily, the Brahman boy blocked it, so the knife stabbed only his hand. The next day the headmaster beat Ram Pal with a stick in front of the whole school.

I always felt some pity for him. In all his life, he was never good to anybody. Not even his brother or sisters. He went to college and lived in Boota Mandi, outside Jalandhar. The Indian National Congress won the election and his Scheduled Castes Federation lost to MLA Sarwan Singh (a member of the legislative assembly who later became foreign minister). When the Congress motor parade passed by, he threw a stone at them. Congress leaders filed a case against him, and he was roughed up for many years and learned his lesson. Then he moved to England and died there due to heavy drinking.

NATURAL DISASTERS

The village suffered many natural disasters. In 1945, the whole village was demolished by torrential rain and floods except for a few brick houses. The mud houses were all destroyed. People rebuilt their houses without removing the mud and debris.

The flood in October 1947 turned out to be one of the worst in history. There were rumors that the government caused it intentionally by letting the water out of Bhakra Dam to save the dam from damage due to heavy rain. All the mud houses were demolished, and the brick houses' walls were cracked, except our house, which stood the test of time. My father's nephew Puran Ram had refused to take the empty plot in 1930 because of a big pit and had threatened to go back to the old village. My uncle Lekh Chand asked my father to exchange plots with Puran Ram and give him ours. My father bought a very cheap kiln that was going out of business. He laid the foundation of the house right at the bottom of the pit, eight feet deep and three feet wide, and built the house. Therefore, the outside walls were so strong that they were not affected by the four-foot-deep flood waters in 1947. I tried to catch a big piece of lumber floating among the other debris and nearly drowned when I slipped.

My distant uncle Lalu Ram had hidden his silver rupees in a pitcher in the ground. Because the foundation of his house wasn't deep enough, the rainwater seeped into the ground and became a fountain right in the middle of the room. With the water pressure, the pitcher moved, and they couldn't find it. My auntie was in a panic looking for the pitcher in the mud. She was worried but didn't want to disclose that she had silver rupees hidden in the ground.

Because of the partition, all our Muslim customers were in camps. We had a lot of finished leather in stock and our store was full. My father asked the workers to store leather in their houses. Their mud houses collapsed on our leather and it was all destroyed. We had a hard time selling it even after cleaning and reprocessing and we suffered a big loss. The village was lacking in education. Many children started their schooling but didn't finish high school due to poverty or the toxic school environment. I was also mediocre in my studies but managed to pass high school. I was viewed as a role model in the village as the first to pass both primary and high school and go to college. I didn't do well at college due to domestic problems but gained enough strength and knowledge to understand my responsibilities and develop some grit. Knowing that I would never succeed in Indian evil society, I made up my mind to leave India and go to the UK. It took me more than a year to get a passport because of fear of my father. I didn't want to tell him that his son wanted to change his orbit. Finally, in 1953, I got my passport and proceeded to the UK, where and I paved the way for my villagers, friends, and other Indian acquaintances to follow me to the new world. I opened the door to better opportunities and a better life for them.

CHAPTER SEVEN

HIGH SCHOOL
1940

After passing primary school (fourth grade), I joined the district board high school on Mahatpur Road in 1940. It was a big relief for me to travel just three quarters of a mile instead of two miles as I had for primary school. The high school was equipped with desks and benches. No one sat on the floor like in primary school. The school was made of red bricks with a huge garden and robust green hedges, a pristine playing field, and a hostel for distant village students. There was nothing but open space between my village and the school, and I could see one from the other. I walked to school through green fields for the next eight years. The farmland was arid, depending on the rain, and uncared-for. This was the only government high school in the whole *tehsil* of Nakodar, and most students traveled by bicycle or on foot within a five-to six-mile radius. There was a private Aryan high school in town for local high-caste Hindu students.

LEARNING ENGLISH
In fifth grade, I started learning English. The English teacher, Dhenu Ram, was a tall, slim man with a cream turban and was a high-caste Brahman. He was first a

Brahman, not first a teacher. He was regarded as a good teacher but was racist. He behaved terribly toward me and a couple of other boys from my community. He used to hit us with a cane but didn't dare to even touch the cane afterward because it had touched us and was therefore polluted. Every day he brought a new cheap cane. I suffered greatly in fifth grade. I felt the cold, familiar feelings I'd felt in primary school. His face haunted my dreams. This teacher's supposedly admirable teaching style was one I didn't happen to admire. The school was known for some tyrannical teachers, but somehow my spirit was lifted as I grew a little older and stronger, and more able to bear the insults as I was hungry for knowledge.

In seventh grade, I learned the Persian language and I still remember poems written by Sheik Shadi, a great poet of that language. I often recite these poems when I'm in a good mood. When I was twelve years old, a British or half-British education inspector came along with the headmaster Mohan Lal to examine the students. I was sitting at the front desk, near the entrance. All the students stood up, paid respects, and welcomed the officer. Suddenly, he looked at me and asked me a history question. It was a history period, the question was "Aram-ko Be-Aram kis ne keya?" ("Who made the ruler Aram uncomfortable?"). I was shocked. The teacher, Mohan Rai, turned pale. Then the inspector repeated the question in a louder voice. I had studied history the night before and without too much frustration, I answered the question. The inspector immediately complimented me by saying *shabash*. He knew the answer was right and I assumed it was correct because of his response. This was an iconic moment for me. My teacher, the headmaster, and the whole class were happy. It was the first time I'd received a compliment in my entire school life, and it came from a non-Indian. Other than that, I had always been discouraged. This was my happiest moment.

LOSING A YEAR

In eighth grade, I became very sick and missed the whole school year. My teacher Lohia Ram and the other Brahman teachers used to scoff at us and call us derogatory names. I think my good name was too good for them. I was a mediocre student, and a few times I was punished by being made to stand on the bench for a long time because I couldn't pronounce *San Francisco* correctly. Another word I couldn't pronounce was *Linlithgow*. But I managed to get into ninth grade.

A fellow from my village, Ram Pal, who was a year behind me, joined my class in eighth grade and we used to sit together at one desk. He was a notorious troublemaker and a spoiled boy, and extravagant because his father had a lot of money. He was a little stronger than me and used to dress in fancy clothes. I wasn't happy about his insulting behavior because he was bossy and dictatorial. I complained to the teacher, Master Sudhir. He told me that if I couldn't stand up to him, then should keep away from him and gave me a different desk to use.

MASTER LAKHAN SINGH

In 1947, Muslims moved into camps and our school was in the center of them. It was swarmed with Muslim people going to Pakistan, so the school was closed, and classes were discontinued for a long time. In ninth and tenth grade, the only teacher I admired was Lakhan Singh. He was the junior headmaster and in charge of classes. He was Sikh, but he was different than other

Sikhs, Hindus, or Muslims. He possessed a small body but a very big heart and used to wear a cream-colored turban, pajamas, and a tunic. In the summer, I saw him wearing short trousers and long white socks up to his knees. He didn't care much about trimming his moustache and beard. He was a good teacher as well as a good human being. He was tough but soft, which made him unpredictable. All the students feared him and, at the same time, respected him. Although he was not smug like the other teachers, he earned a reputation because of this. He was brimming with fortitude and looked like a proper teacher. He believed his students had only one agenda; to get an education. To this end, he offered his profuse talents to his students wholeheartedly.

He was committed to making a difference in students' lives. He became an icon to them, and no one was more respected and revered than Master Lakhan Singh. He was near enough to being a Guru. He galvanized students into action, leading to improvement in their studies, so nothing would deter them from success. His story is not complete without a mention of his favorite phrase, "Chalk and talk." He ordered students to solve algebra questions or geometry propositions on a big blackboard, and at the same time, he expected them to talk. He always advised distant village students to join boarding school and helped them in their studies after school hours and in the early morning before school time. His sublime and noble motive was to achieve a full, one hundred percent passing result for the school, and he did because he cared about the reputation of the school and his students.

Unfortunately, it was the time of the partition of the

country and everything was disrupted in 1947–48. More people were worried about their lives than their studies, and the schools' results were the worst in history. My result was delayed, but I barely graduated from high school. My parents were happy because I was the first boy from the family and second boy from the whole village to pass high school. I wasn't happy at all because of my very low marks, and I wished I had failed. At the same time, I was happy, as I was finally getting the chance to get away from these horrible, racist teachers.

High School (1945)

CHAPTER EIGHT

SHIV RAJ

I stared at him with wonder and amazement. He was a handsome, tall, and perfect young man, standing in the burning heat of the sun, in front of the main gate of my father's workplace. He was bewildered, trying to ascertain whether he was in the right place. I thought he must be some government official. He came straight to our place through the fields from nearby train station. It was the end of April 1943 and I was twelve years old then, doing my schoolwork in the seventh grade. I told my father about the visitor who was working nearby. My father looked and smiled, shouting, "Babu ji! Come in. Don't stand there." As the work floor was wet and dirty, my father told him to be very careful. He instructed me to bring bedsheets and a pillow from home to make him comfortable. At that time, we didn't have chairs in our house or workplace. Instead we used folding and moveable beds for seating and to receive visitors.

My father introduced Shiv Raj to me. He was the brother-in-law of my elder brother Shenker Dutt and had come to see his elder sister Jai Rani. I often heard about him from my brother but had never met him. He was twenty-one years old then, with thick black hair, carefully combed and parted slightly to the right corner of his head. His nose was big and pointed, flanked by his big eyes and a lot of impressive features. He was neatly dressed and wore polished Bata shoes and trousers with a striped shirt. As a student, he was in his second year at Randhir College, Kapurthala, and the state capital. At that time, he was the only college student I knew because college was a new thing for villagers. He won the State Maharaja scholarship by scoring the highest marks on the high school matriculation exam and was invited to attend the college for further studies (it was the only college in the state at that time). His parents were not willing to send him without the scholarship due to the high fees and other costs. After finishing two years of studies at Kapurthala, he went to Doaba College in Jalandhar, and that same year he was married to an uneducated girl named Bhagwati.

After graduating in 1945, he was hired in Shimla, a hill station and summer capital of India, as a senior clerk in the Ministry of Transport, a government department of India. Neither he nor his parents knew anyone in Shimla, and they couldn't afford the hotel and other expenses required to start a new life there. Finally, a friend from a nearby village called Pandori arranged for him to stay with strangers for a month before he found his own home. His place was down the hill near Annandale grounds, quite far from offices on the mall, and he settled down there for several years. While he was in service in Shimla, he helped many poor boys from his community by giving them free lodging for a month or so until they got jobs and could stand on their own feet. One of them was my distant cousin Ram Dyal.

AN ONWARD JOURNEY

After the partition of India in August 1947, Shiv Raj was transferred to New Delhi and promoted to the next rank. He found accommodation in Karol Bagh in Delhi again, a place with two small rooms and a kitchen. From Delhi, he used to come to his village to see his parents and then to my house every year, sometimes twice a year. Traveling from Delhi to Punjab was not difficult due to improvements in communication. It was also easy for my father and brother to pay a visit to Shiv Raj on their long journey to Kanpur for business purposes. Shiv Raj was very much respected by my father and brother and his in-laws and other relatives because of his education and government job. In return, Shiv Raj also looked up to my father, relying on him for good advice and help with other family matters, and they became very close. After a few years, a minor problem regarding education cropped up between Shiv Raj and his wife, which was quite common in those days, but it was aggravated by their close relatives. Soon it reached my father's ears. He was hurt by Shiv Raj's behavior and lost interest in him. As I was growing up, I visited Delhi off and on and heard Shiv Raj's complaints against his close relatives.

WELL-EDUCATED AND RESPONSIBLE

He was a responsible person, a good father, a good educator, and a man of vision. I was a friend to him and a frequent visitor. Whenever I was in Delhi, I tried to spend more time with him and his family. Many times, I saw how hard he strived to look after his young children, so they got to school in time, were in good health, dressed in neat and clean clothes, and were properly fed. One time we were sleeping outside his house in Moti Bagh, and in the early morning the milkman came and went as everyone was sleeping. He got up quickly and ran after the milkman, even losing his loincloth (dhoti), as there were no other shops to get milk nearby. I often saw him make toast for his children and fix the collars of their shirts, so they looked neat. He did his best to educate them so they could live a comfortable life. He did a lot more for his children than a typical good father.

He built a house in Ashok Vihar, Delhi, for his children's comfort, but by this time, he was getting old. He had seen many ups and downs and was used to living in any kind of environment. He had gained so much and missed so much. No one is perfect. We all miss some things. This is life, but in his old age he was suffering. He began to complain to me in every letter and ask me what he had done wrong. Most of his children were turning against him. I had also noticed tension in the house and didn't like it. There were a lot of negative outside influences on the children. They were thinking more about themselves and less about their father. They were lacking lot of wisdom and morality. But who could tell them? They were big-time officers, suffering from the common Delhi disease of egotism and greed, and wanted the best they could get?

Their frequent immoral actions and ill-treatment hurt him very much. He had come from a small village, and in many ways, he was still a true villager. He had changed through time, but not enough to understand his children. He did his best to make them college-literate, but failed to give them a full, valued, ethical education. We argued and complained to each other. Sometimes he said I was wrong, and other times I said he was wrong. I felt very sad and became concerned that the same thing could happen to me. However, I was sure that my children will have had a different kind of education, had seen bad days, and will have appreciated what their mother and father had done for them despite all their hardships.

His children bought or rented their own dwellings, and after his wife's death, he was left in his house unattended. He didn't know how to cook, as he'd never cooked in his life. He wasn't inclined to hire someone. It wasn't that he was miserly, just old and lonely. Sometimes he admired his elder brother Jai Raj and the way his children took care of him. He ran back and forth to Punjab to pass the time and find company. And finally, he made his mistake. He was suffering from bronchitis, and when it was severe, he used an electric breathing machine. In the villages, sometimes electricity or other utilities weren't readily available or stopped working at any time. It was a severe attack; he had no power for the machine, and he breathed his last. Without him, I didn't like Delhi. His children took no interest in their father, similarly to the attention one would give to someone who is not a relative. They were Shiv Raj's children, but not like Shiv Raj. He possessed wisdom and virtues that none of his children, grandchildren, or immediate relatives inherited, such as putting his arm around your neck or waist to make you feel welcome in his house. Truth, love, sympathy, and faith in each other had been the cement between us as we continued to nurture our friendship. His efforts and influences inspired me and other people.

His letters were written by hand in ink. In most cases, they became the seal of a long personal relationship. Because we were intimate friends, he always wrote interesting letters concerning his well-being and things happening in the family, which gave me great pleasure to read. These letters heightened my interest in him. Even more than me, my wife Nasib Kaur looked forward to his mail. She asked me to read the letters again and again until she grasped every word. We enjoyed hearing from him. His letters to me were the longest in the whole correspondence.

He had great charm and was always interested in exchanging views, but much more in establishing personal relationships. He argued back and forth and fought against my positions with a passion. He didn't conceal his desires from me. His thinking was fluid. Most people like to be proven right, and so he was. He had more than an influence on me; he was authoritative to me and it was fed by his service and sympathy. It was Shiv Raj who forced me to attend college. Otherwise, I had given up because of my very low marks on the matriculation exam. He retained my respect through tenderness and patience, and I always sought his approval. I was happy when he agreed with me and we did everything we could to stay connected. He cared for me and that was enough. He was a motherly person to me, which was comforting to me and constituted a true and valuable friendship. I miss him very much and have never found anyone to replace him with whom I can talk heart-to-heart and freely. He left his memoirs for me to cherish forever.

Shiv Raj and his wife

CHAPTER NINE

MY VISIT TO SHIMLA
1945

Ram Dyal's father, Blasa Rai (my distant uncle) was going to Shimla to see his son and Shiv Raj. Shiv Raj wrote a letter to my father asking him to send me to Shimla along with Uncle Blasa Rai for a vacation. This was my first long-distance train journey. From Nakodar we went to Ludhiana, took the train to Ambala, and changed trains in Kalka, in the foothills. The train reached Kalka in early morning, around 4:00 a.m. I slept all the way to Kalka. When I woke up, I saw a big thick black wall facing me, but I was still half asleep. I was scared and wondered what was happening—what was going on? Where were we?

As the morning fog cleared, I noticed huge, grassy green hills covered in trees and bushes. We changed to a small train on a small track, only two and a half feet wide, with a very powerful engine. It took us all day to travel about sixty-two miles through a hundred tunnels of various sizes. It was a steep journey all the way, and at some corners, the train hardly traveled five miles per hour. The scenery was breathtaking. We came across myriad types of trees, bushes, rocks, and mountains along the way. We had a long wait at a train station called Tara Devi. I could see all the tall, important government office buildings and hotels on the mall and elsewhere at their high altitude in Shimla. Finally, in the late evening we reached the city.

It was so different from the plains of Punjab. There were English people with suits and neckties. There were lots of big and small monkeys sitting everywhere on trees, roads, and office buildings. There were rickshaws pulled by two men, looking very unstable. The mall was perfectly clean and beautiful. To escape the scorching heat of Delhi, the capital city, the government offices and officers moved to this hill city of Shimla, situated at a higher altitude.

It was my first time encountering English people. I was very shy and couldn't look at them, especially the women, because they were minimally but neatly dressed compared to Indians. The British appeared well-mannered, cultured, and well-dressed. I was living in a different environment compared to Punjab, where the whole area was ravaged by the caste system and its hate. I didn't know anyone here except my relatives, and I felt so free, full of vigor and enthusiasm. This was the first time I'd felt happy since beginning primary school at the age of five. I spent a month in Shimla with Shiv Raj and his wife. He didn't have extensive accommodations, so my uncle and I shared one big bed at nighttime. I used to go out with my uncle late in the morning and roam around among the big bushes and deodar trees. The trees were so healthy, dense, and tall that it was hard to see the sky. A few times my uncle lost his turban looking up into the tops of the trees. There were a lot of monkeys, and we were afraid and very careful not to disturb them. There was a roar of water flowing down from the slopes and mountains.

AN ONWARD JOURNEY

The noise went on all the time and we got used to it. Within one month, I was well familiar with the surroundings, roads, and the mall in Shimla.

About eighteen months after my first visit, I returned to Shimla. This time, I accompanied Shiv Raj's father Dev Rai. He was enthusiastic to see Shimla and the offices where his son was employed. Shiv Raj was living a hundred miles away from his family and home. Dev Rai was like a father-in-law to me. He was my wife's uncle and had raised her like his own daughter after the death of her beloved father. My wife and I were and remain sincerely obliged to Dev Rai and his wife for the rest of our lives. This was his first long-distance journey outside his very backward village.

He was a highly respected man in his village. The villagers looked to him for advice and help in their time of need. He was the only person in the village who owned a few acres of land and had educated his two sons, Shiv Raj and Jai Raj. This was a big achievement and victory for a family in the days when education was not readily available to poor, low-caste people. He was a very simple and fair-skinned person with good features. He liked to wear a white dhoti and turban, which was considered very old-fashioned in a city like Shimla, the summer capital of India, full of English folks. Dev Rai was very anxious to see the big office buildings where his son was working, but Shiv Raj was not excited to take him there to meet his colleagues as Dev Rai was wearing village clothes and was uneducated. Shiv Raj was feeling some sense of humiliation about taking his old-fashioned father to his office. However, we visited Ram Dyal's office a few times since he didn't care much about his status. We knew other boys who were working in neighboring offices. We made it our routine to visit all of them in turn and since we were visitors, they all treated us nicely with tea, coffee, *laddu*, and *burfi*. In fact, I started gaining weight due to the rich food.

We often went for a stroll and sometimes we heard some women singing sweet songs. Dev Rai was fascinated with these voices. He often sat quietly on a rock to listen to the melodious songs and wondered who and where the person was. There were dense jungles and we never came across any dangerous animals except for monkeys. For Dev Rai, this was a completely new world, totally different from the poor village life. I had an uncontrollable desire to see Shimla and its surroundings, so walking didn't tire me. The deodar-scented breeze that blew down from the cool wooded slopes refreshed my mind and gave me serene comfort and enjoyment.

I was very fond of Hindi movies and songs. One time, Shiv Raj took me to a movie called *Shah Jahan* with melodious songs sung by the late singer Kundan Lal Sehgal from Jalandhar. Sometimes when I was at home, I used to play with their little child, Lajwanti. Bhagmati was expecting another child and didn't like to go outside, especially up and down the hills, so she used to send me to the sweets shop about a quarter mile away. She often asked me to take the child with me, so she had enough free time to cook and do other chores. The child was in poor health and I often refrained from doing so, but there was sometimes no way out as we needed cooked food. There was a nice big bungalow near the shop where I could hear the hit songs being played on the radio. So, I made a point to go to the shop at an exact time and listen to the songs. Sometimes I walked very close to the bungalow, sat on the grass, and pretended to play with the child while my mind was focused on my favorite songs. As I had the kid with me, nobody minded me sitting there.

On the weekends, I toured and enjoyed my visits to Chotta Shimla, Jutogh, and other small villages around Shimla with my relatives and their friends. Shiv Raj had a brown wool jacket custom made for me and it was the first jacket I'd ever owned, at the age of fourteen. I liked that jacket so much that I kept it for a long time. Shiv Raj and his numerous friends, all from the same community, were staying in a row of quarters consisting of two rooms and a small attached yard near the Annandale grounds. Annandale was a racecourse and football ground, a big open space in the middle of the big mountains below the mall.

I met Om Puri from Nawanshahr, Punjab. He was also a graduate of Jalandhar College. The other boys were high school graduates, all employed in government offices as clerks. They all used to get together on the weekends at Shiv Raj's place, and I became acquainted with each of them. Some belonged to very poor households and had to send money to their parents every month from their small incomes. Around the Annandale grounds there were a lot of fruit trees. Two of the boys, on their way to Shiv Raj's place, used to break the branches of the fruit trees. On their return journey, late at night, they used to pick the fruits from the broken branches in the pitch dark. They lived on these fruits in order to send a good part of their salaries home to their needy parents.

During these visits to Shimla, I became very well acquainted with Shiv Raj and his family, and soon became very close to him. I was married to his cousin's sister, who was ten years younger than him. Shiv Raj treated me like his own brother-in-law, and his children were respectful to me. My visit to Shimla proved a big turning point in the life of a small and backward village boy. I was inspired in many ways and it was my strong desire to see nature and the world and enjoy my life.

CHAPTER TEN

OUR WEDDING
1947

I was betrothed as early as eight years of age. In India, betrothal is an arrangement purely between the parents, in which the children have no consent or awareness. This engagement is a promise the parents initiate between the boy and the girl to join them in marriage.

I have a faint recollection of the engagement. One evening I was dressed in new clothes and made to sit under a shady tree in the front yard of my big house, on a rough new carpet. People from the village gathered and sang songs. My mother was the first to perform rituals, and then her other friends, relatives, and neighbors followed. Finally, sweets were distributed to the people. It was a small ceremony and lasted about four hours. The matchmaker (*bachola*), who happened to be a distant cousin of my father (called Lala Ji), was sent to the girl's village with some presents for her.

Now, I was fully booked to marry a girl who lived twenty-five miles away in a remote village. After my engagement in 1939, I became more important and visible to the girl's parents and relatives. My family had four brothers. My elder brother Schenker Dutt was already married to Jai Rani, the cousin of the girl I was engaged to, whose name was Nasib Kaur. He and his wife initiated all the matchmaking events. My parents used to visit their relatives and the girl's folks used to visit Nakodar to see their daughter or niece. They had seen me often and liked me. My parents were fond of the girl. She was about my age and quite healthy. So, long before my engagement, both of our families knew each other.

My father-in-law, Veryam Chand, died soon after our engagement. He died in Calcutta on a business trip and his body was brought back to his village and cremated there. My mother-in-law was left with three young daughters. They were living with their uncle's family in a big house. Uncle Dev Rai and his wife were good at supporting people. They had a few acres of land and some business deals. My mother-in-law was a shareholder in the land. She was a very hardworking woman and after the death of her husband, she raised her daughters with the help of her brother-in-law Dev Rai, his wife, and their two sons, Jai Raj and Shiv Raj.

In those days, girls were considered a burden or liability to the family. Therefore, the sooner they got rid of the burden, the better. Boys were considered an asset to the family. For my mother-in-law, her daughters were a constant source of worry. My father Amar Chand was also very concerned about the family's welfare. To add fuel to the fire, my prospective wife developed some sort of migraine headache that affected her eyes. She was in pain all the time. There were no qualified doctors available in the village or nearby towns. The family wasn't wealthy enough to go to the big city to find a qualified doctor. She was treated by a village witch doctor who damaged her eyes for the rest of her life. Now her folks were more worried that my parents might change their minds and refuse to accept her.

I used to hear about her welfare when her folks were visiting my house. They always criticized me for my poor health, and I didn't like to hear that. I used to hide or walk away whenever I saw them, and they complained to my father and insisted on seeing me. Their daughter was growing up and there was talk of our impending marriage. Finally, the date of the wedding was set for the following year. But before it took place, I fell ill. I was sick for a few months and lost a lot of weight. I couldn't even attend school. I was thirteen years old at that time, in 1944.

Back then, sugar and cloth weren't readily available, and everything was rationed due to the Second World War. If one wanted more sugar or cloth for a wedding or some other purpose, they had to apply to the local government for authorization. My in-laws applied for sugar and cloth and they were granted permission to buy some. Because I was weak and recovering from my illness, my father asked my in-laws to postpone the date of the wedding. But there were no easy answers, and he knew that changing the date would cause a lot of confusion and problems with the local government officials. I remember him taking me to my school to request a grant of leave from the headmaster for a week. The teacher laughed and told my father to save my life before thinking of my marriage.

The wedding date was drawing closer and my father tried to avoid a lot of the rituals because of my poor health. But the local women insisted and smeared my body all over with a turmeric paste to change the color of my skin—what little body I had left. I was miserable, feeble, and looked like a skeleton. I had developed a flat and insipid appearance and was infinitely awkward and clumsy. One mistake was made after another, and I wasn't happy at all. Our village was small at that time and all the villagers knew my in-laws. All the men and boys joined in the marriage party. We took the train to Jalandhar and then to Phagwara. We had a lot of time on our hands, and according to the plan, we were to reach my in-laws' village in the evening. So, my father never thought of hiring even a tonga and made me walk with the rest of the wedding party. I regretted this fact all my life. We stopped to rest outside Phagwara under a shady banyan tree, then proceeded slowly to the village. I was in no shape for anything, let alone getting married.

As we approached the village, crowds of my father's old friends turned out to greet us. The marriage festivities were underway, and we received a very warm welcome with a band to lead us to our big tent, which was set up in the front yard of a house in the neighborhood. There were about a hundred people there and my in-laws tried to accommodate everybody with portable beds (charpoys) and sheets. The whole village was at our wedding. They were so enthusiastic about the marriage and they comforted us. My father refused to perform any rituals after the big dinner as I was sleeping. I remember someone carrying me to the place before I woke up to meet the household.

The next morning, I was again told to get up early, about five o'clock, for the actual marriage ceremony, the *phere* (ceremony around a burning fire). I can picture myself even today performing the *phere*, or seven steps. We walked together around the fire, promising mutual devotion and fidelity. This ceremony was set for before sunrise. The letter was a prophetic indication of a good union or marriage. I was sitting on the wedding dais and a small fire was burning in front of it. A canopy-style artificial structure had been built in the front yard of the residence to cover the ceremony. My parents, brother, and family friends and the bride's people were all there to witness the occasion. It was a little chilly.

Soon some of Nasib Kaur's girlfriends and female relatives, dressed in brilliant *salwar kameez*, brought the bride out of her house and made her sit beside me. This was the first time I saw her, covered all over in bridal clothes. Her face was covered, too, and she could hardly see. She was strong and sturdy and spent much of the ceremony gazing down at the floor, her hands heavily hennaed with a design befitting a newly married girl. Her folks were pouring butter over the fire to keep it burning; it was a good smell all around. The village priest from my own community was doing his work, chanting mantras and performing rituals. Soon the ceremony was over, and we were married. It was March 1944 and I was only thirteen years old. She went into her house and I returned to my tent with my parents and other family members to change my clothes. A lot of my father's friends and relatives came in the early morning to attend the wedding. Most of them knew my father through business contacts or friendship. We weren't strangers to each other.

We had a very good lunch and we all competed for fun to see how much butter, sugar, and chapatis we could consume. In the evening, after a small snack, we planned to leave with the bride, of course. But my in-laws refused and wanted us to stay another night although it wasn't customary. Because both sides had known each other for a long time, my in-laws insisted. There was a lot of food in stock and the tents were already there. Some members of the party left that evening, but most of us stayed.

The next morning after breakfast, we departed from the village. The bride was wailing uncontrollably. She slowly marched with her friends toward the waiting tonga that would take us to the Phagwara train station. This time the bride was sitting beside me, but I never lifted my eyes because I was too shy. She was covered as usual due to purdah (seclusion of women from public view). We came home in the evening by train. My mother and neighbors performed a ceremony to welcome her. She seemed familiar with my house as she had seen my parents when they visited her house and had heard all the stories of my family and our surroundings for many years. What she didn't know was that we had a big yard and plenty of space to live and that we weren't poor. She was happy to find that we lived less than half a mile from the train station and she could go places without much difficulty. She lived in my house for two nights with Shiv Raj's wife Bhagmati and some other friends, and they all stayed in one room.

Then she left for her village. This was my wedding to a girl I never even saw or spoke to before or after the wedding day. All I was sure of was that she had two feet for moving about and plenty of big clothes. I can't blame anyone because these were established customs among poor families of my community. Weddings were costly, and arranging marriages was just a matter of convenience and opportunity. There was no concern about the boy and girl because they were too young to live together.

I heard regularly from my parents about her welfare. About three years later, in March 1947, my father abruptly told me that he had arranged for my *muklaba* (final marriage event) and told me to get my clothes ready as we had to catch an early train. I was in tenth grade and busy with my studies, but my father had no clue about their importance. He lacked comprehension of the depth of the problem at that time. All I knew was that my household needed some help because my sisters had gotten married and left to live with their husbands. My parents and I, Shenker Dutt, and his wife Jai Rani all went to her village and stayed there overnight, and the next day we came back with my wife, Nasib Kaur. We also brought her other people, her cousin-brother Shiv Raj and his wife Bhagmati. They stayed with us for a few days, then went home, leaving her behind with me.

Rest assured that we were too nervous to face each other. We were certainly too shy. We gradually began getting to know each other and were eventually able to speak freely together. We were the same age, sixteen. We were just young, immature, and foolish kids. She stayed in my house with me for sixteen days. During this time, I learned that by nature she was a very simple girl, with a humble upbringing in a remote village, but she had inviolable moral standards. Although she wasn't educated, she earned my respect. She was wise. There was a lot of chemistry between us to join her thoughts and life with mine. I don't think she wanted to go back to her village so soon, but what could she or I do to fight all these old customs? Her aunt came and took her away from me. She asked me to come to her village the following week to see her, but that didn't happen.

CHAPTER ELEVEN

NASIB KAUR AND HER SETBACKS

My wife Nasib Kaur was a remote village girl, born in 1932, the oldest in the family, and never went to school. It was an arranged marriage by none other than my parents. My father knew the good family because my elder brother Shenker Dutt was already married to my wife's cousin, Jai Rani.

She was raised in a small village by her uncle and aunt, people with old wisdom. She inherited this wisdom from her uncle as well as the strength of determination. She was recognized for her compassion and care. Since she didn't go out to town or anywhere else because of her eye trouble, she remained strictly a village girl and learned how to do every domestic task and take responsibility for the house. She also remained free of caste prejudice and untouchability before our marriage. Later in life, my children and I became the beneficiaries of her good habits and deeds, and she turned her husband, a man of small dreams, into a man of vision. Her gentle manners and air of repose didn't disguise her lovely spirit. She had amazing potential for goodness. She was indeed a perfect housewife and a perfect hostess. She had no education, but in sense and vigor, she was much more than educated. She was always a humble person with charismatic grace. She expressed herself in words with tenderness and talent. She always weighed her words before speaking.

SETBACKS
Nasib Kaur suffered many setbacks at an early age after our engagement in 1939. She had lost her father Veryam Chand when she was only nine or ten years old and had two younger sisters, but no brother. One tragedy followed another: she suffered with severe migraine headaches for a long time and lost her eyesight when a phony village doctor damaged her eyes.

Her mother raised her daughters with the help of her beloved auntie, uncle, Dev Rai and their two sons, Jai Raj and Shiv Raj. For this act of kindness, she felt obliged to them until the last day of her life. She was very obedient and respectful to her cousin-brothers, whom she considered more than real brothers, and respected them all her life. As a matter of high regard and honor, she never lifted her eyes in front of them.

Not making eye contact with her brothers or cousins was considered a standard respectful norm for girls at that time. My wife never called them by their names, always referring to them as *bera ji* (dear brother) as a matter of respect. One time she told me that she could tell by their voices who was who because she never tried to lift her eyes to look at them. These predominant, unique, and sacred inner qualities were a good measurement of a pious and perfect human being who was rich in heart, which created a lot of respect and love in my heart for her.

DOMESTIC PROBLEMS

After our wedding in March 1947, she again suffered with her eyes and visited the eye hospital in Ludhiana regularly for three or four years, but it was no use. We didn't find a competent, experienced doctor. She was a great believer in God and always said a prayer before going to the doctor, asking why she was destined to suffer. What had she done wrong to deserve this? Even in my house, she found no consolation because we had no money as I wasn't working; I was just a freshman in college. We were both dependent on my parents for our daily living. She did all the domestic work, cleaning, cooking, and milking the cows. She drew water from the village well with a huge bucket. She was answerable to all in the family. But they ignored all of that. She spent more than half of her time at her mother's place after our wedding. At the time, it was a life of chronic suffering and the future looked dim. Destiny must have been guiding our actions. I often fell into deep thought during that time. Life was tough and there was no easy solution. We weren't much of a burden on my father, and he maintained that her eye problems were her fate (kismet), which distressed me and surprised me. I disliked my position for the next two years as I thought over the problem. It was a time of realization and a need for me to act.

GOD HELPS THOSE WHO HELP THEMSELVES

Finally, God accepted her prayers and later, I managed to reach Scotland in April 1954. But before leaving home, I made sure she had a passport to follow me to Scotland. My father, however, was adamant about not sending her to me in a foreign country until I had a house of my own, especially since I now had a firstborn child, Kamlesh. He made many excuses not to send my wife and child. In fact, he missed me very much and wanted me to come back. I didn't want to do that because of my precarious situation and suffering. I wasn't willing to listen to all the excuses and I wanted my wife and child with me. Finally, I surrendered to my adamant but sincere father and bought a house after a year and a half. It was only then when my father finally permitted my wife to join me in Scotland.

My Wife's First Picture
Nasib Kaur, Age 19 (1950)

CHAPTER TWELVE

MY HELPLESSNESS

To fulfill the old traditions, my wife had gone to her mother's house with her aunt and was expecting me to show up there. I was thinking about her all the time and was feeling very sad. It was so hard to focus on my studies. I was anxious to see her, but permission to go had to come from my father. Months passed, but my father never bothered to tell me to go and see my wife. Such was life in those days. I was too timid to ask my father about it.

Soon news started trickling into the villages about the Hindu-Muslim riots. This was in 1947, at the time of the partition in India. In some big cities, Hindus and Muslims were fighting and the riots spread to Punjab. In the coming months, June and July 1947, things started getting bad and the religious war spread to the villages. People were scared to go out. Anyone who left the house wasn't sure to come back.

RELIGIOUS FIGHTING
In August 1947, Muslims started leaving their houses with only a few belongings and gathering in camps to go to Pakistan. Hindus and Sikhs were

attacking Muslims, and Muslims were attacking them. I wasn't sure that my wife and her family were safe because her village was predominantly Muslim. They weren't sure if we had survived the riots. Then immigration started; Hindus and Sikhs in Pakistan began coming to India, and Muslims in India began leaving for Pakistan. The refugees settled in schools, camps, and religious buildings. Schools were closed for students and teachers. Lives were in danger, and it was impossible to get out safely.

Finally, at the turn of the year, things started to quiet down. There were no trains and no buses. My father traveled on foot in the darkness and stopped to rest with friends on the road before he reached the village twenty-five miles away. It took him two days. We were worried, but after a few days, he came back with my wife and her mother.

About four months passed happily, and then my wife's eyes started giving her trouble again. There were no qualified doctors in my town, so I started inquiring about one. Finally, Mohat Ram, the family's regular hakim, told us to go to the eye hospital in Ludhiana, about thirty-five miles away. We kept going there for three or four years for checkups, once or twice a month, and a couple of times she was admitted to the hospital. I was studying in college then, and I had no income.

A DIFFICULT TIME

The conditions in the house with the blended family were not good. The eye doctor had advised my wife to keep away from smoke and dust. But at home, family members still expected her to do all sorts of typical domestic work like cooking, cleaning, and sweeping the floor of the house and big yard. In those days, we didn't have electricity or gas for cooking, so we used other types of fuel that were readily available, like cakes made from cow dung, waste wood, or leaves, which produced a lot of smoke. I was in a bind. I'd fallen behind a year in college due to my illness. At the same time, I was preparing to sit for examinations again. Those days were full of frustration. No income, no money, but lots of worries and problems. It was yet another definite low period in my life.

My brother's wife, my wife's cousin, was twelve years older than my wife, a beautiful and hardworking woman who oversaw the house. She was industrious, very fond of making cakes from cow dung and shredded bark. She used to sell these cakes to pottery makers and others. She spent half the day making cakes, which was very hard, dirty, and smelly work. We could easily afford to buy this fuel, but she was used to this kind of life. She used to take her daughter with her and taught her how to make fuel cakes instead of sending her to school. She detested my wife and me for living free and not doing any work. She was quite right that I wasn't earning any money, while my brother was a hardworking person.

But my wife always maintained that she was left alone in the house to milk the cows early in the morning, then clean the house and cook food for my brother's children to take to school. This work was enough to deserve a couple of meals a day. We had no children then. My wife's eye problem, our lack of money and support from our parents, and the arguments among the family were driving me mad. To keep peace in the house, I suggested that my wife go home to her mother. She declined, saying that her uncle and aunt would think the reason she came back was that I put her out of the house. She didn't want to leave me because I was the only person looking after her welfare. So, we decided that I would take her to her village and talk to her uncle and aunt. Instead of going to Nakodar on the weekends, I would visit her village. Her mother didn't have money since she was a widow, and her uncle and aunt depended on their sons for their living. They had a few acres of farmland to support their basic needs. Her mother used to keep a few hens and sell eggs to pay the fare to take her to the hospital (Ludhiana) and cover other needs. My wife was an uneducated village girl with very weak eyesight, and it was difficult to go to the hospital in the busy city. I wasn't so keen on my studies due to these domestic and financial troubles. I started taking a day off from college whenever she had an appointment with the eye doctor. Sometimes I met her on the train, and other times I met her at the Ludhiana train station before walking the mile and a half to the hospital.

My wife's eyes were not improving. The doctors told her to take cod liver oil, but we did not have money to buy such expensive things. We did not have money for medicine. We both were grown up and we did not want too much of a burden on anybody. I cut my expenses to minimum and started dodging my parents and decided to give up my studies, so I can save some rupees to buy medicine and other necessary items for my wife. My parents and other members wanted her to do all the housework, but they did not want to look after her illness. Life was very dull and miserable.

MY PLAN TO GO ABROAD
One day in town, I met Mohat Ram's nephew Sat

Bhushan, a friend from my school days who was selling juices and other goods in his father's shop after passing his matriculation exam. Like me, he wasn't doing any constructive work and was fed up. He talked about the possibility of going abroad. I thought he was joking, and I had no clue what he wanted to do. After meeting with him a few times, he convinced me that going to England was the only solution for us to survive. He wanted me to accompany him. A few months later, he left for England after giving me all the instructions to apply for a passport etc. Simply hearing the instructions made me feel ecstatic. I felt it was a godsend that had happened at just the right time.

Knowing that I'd lost interest in my studies, Shenker Dutt advised me to seek employment in Delhi as a clerk. I refused because I believed I wouldn't earn enough to support myself and my wife. I asked my father and brother to let me work in our warehouse in Hansi (near Delhi), but my brother didn't want me to go there; he had his own plans. I was still residing in Jalandhar, pretending to attend college there. Now, I was staying with my brother-in-law Kirpa Chand in Boota Mandi, a leather market outside Jalandhar. I started borrowing small amounts of money from him, knowing that he would easily get reimbursed by my father. He never refused and never asked me where I was spending the money.

This was the right time. In Boota Mandi, I wasn't far from the civil courts in Jalandhar, and I started inquiring about application forms for my passport.

CHAPTER THIRTEEN

AUGUST 15, 1947

August 15, 1947 is India's Independence Day and was the day of partition of Indian soil between Indian Hindus and Pakistani Muslims. It was an auspicious and happy day for many, but it was doomsday for some unfortunate people who lost their loved ones as well as everything they'd worked hard for all their lives. For the downtrodden and poor, freedom had no real meaning. They were slaves and outcasts before the partition and remained slaves after the partition. They were slaves under foreign rule then, and even now they are slaves under the rule of corrupt, powerful, obstinate, and orthodox Hindus and Sikhs in India and Muslims in Pakistan.

THE SUFFERING OF THE POOR

Rich and powerful Hindus, Muslims, and Sikhs fled India and Pakistan long before August 15, 1947. It was the peasants of these groups, the so-called untouchables who had no choice but to stay and suffer on both sides of India and Pakistan in the hands of the barbaric elite.

The area surrounding my hometown of Nakodar, Punjab, had a large Muslim population of aristocrats and other powerful people. It was a stronghold of Muslims. They were sure the Nakodar area would remain part of Pakistan because they had the majority.

Muslims and Hindus were threatening property and safety in big cities like Calcutta, Bombay, and Delhi. There were reports of murder and arson, and the news of these heinous acts reached the neighboring states, including Punjab. Every evening, we heard the loud chants of "Allahu Akbar" ("God is the Greatest") from gangs of Muslims. They were contemptuous and determined to exterminate non-Muslims. These religious fanatics succeeded in widening the gulf and poisoning the relations between communities. The atmosphere was charged with tension and tempers were running high between the religious groups. The communal exploiters and demagogues successfully played on the feelings and sentiments of the masses and swayed them to communal passion. They spread panic through various acts of violence.

All were afraid and unsure of what was to come. We were vulnerable as we were living in the open and in a small community. Rumors spread of an attack on Nakodar, and we heard that Muslim gangs were going to burn Dana Mandi Nakodar (the grain market), only half a mile from my tiny village. Dana Mandi was a big square of double-story buildings made of red bricks. There were shops on the ground floor and families were living upstairs. Women and children gathered bricks on the rooftops in hopes of repelling the attackers, and men brought weapons to protect themselves and their families. Everyone was in a panic as they heard the war chants. At night we stood guard, expecting an assault to occur at any time. The air was thick with tension. Those were very dark and difficult days.

The next day, there were unbelievable reports that Nakodar and its surrounding areas were part of India, not part of Pakistan. We saw Muslims from Nakodar and the neighboring villages leaving in a rush and gathering in camps on Mahatpur Road, a five-mile stretch between Nakodar and Mahatpur. Within a day or two, this road was loaded with Muslims. They were thinking that after a week they would go to Pakistan, their dream land created by their beloved leader, Mr. Mohammed Ali Jinnah. But their dream was just a dream; they were misled, and the hopeful days became disappointing days. The train delayed for a month, and they were stranded in camps, starving and living in misery. They were running out of cash, food, and other necessities. They were dirty, and disease was spreading rapidly. Frequently the sick was abandoned, left to die on the dirty road. They left many corpses behind. Even the weather didn't cooperate with the campers and there were floods. We were living near the camp and felt sorry for them. The promise of paradise by their Muslim leader Jinnah turned into hell for these poor people. Their life had become quite an ordeal.

One day a man from the camp who used to transport our goods wanted to leave his holy Quran and other expensive items with my father, but my father refused as we were not sure of our own lives. We gave him a lot of fodder for his dying bullock, which he loved as his own child.

KNOWLEDGE ABOUT RELIGION
During this period, all the things that happened had a great impact on my young life. I lost faith in human beings. I lost trust in people, and for a while, I lost trust in God. I witnessed so many kinds of beastly acts

committed by Hindus, Sikhs, and Muslims, who murdered and raped innocent women. My cry was, why did God create such monstrous people? I was exasperated and became emotional. How low could a human go in treating another human being so ruthlessly? This was an act of savagery, not humanity, and ironically enough, these very people claimed themselves as a super caste or gods. To me, they weren't even human beings.

One day, two upstanding young Muslim men from the camp went to cut some corn from their own field because their animals were hungry. I was there for the same purpose in the next field. I warned them that they shouldn't have come. Soon after I left them in the cornfield, I heard cries. A group of Sikhs with daggers killed those innocent unarmed men. Then they came after me, and luckily, I was within my village limits. They saw me arrive in the streets and walked away. I wondered about the Sikh guru. Guru Nanak had never taught them to kill innocent unarmed men. And now, killings of innocent Muslims, Hindus, and Sikhs were happening all over India and Pakistan.

During the riots, some Muslim villagers in my district didn't go to the camps. Instead, they stayed in their houses because they were strong and equipped to fight any danger posed by the Hindus and Sikhs. They stayed in their village until they were certain the train had arrived to take them to Pakistan. A group of Sikh militants attacked them a few times but were unsuccessful. Finally, the day came when the Muslims left the village. Before leaving their homes, they emptied their stocks of grain in the center of their living rooms, then sprinkled cow blood and put pieces of dead animals on top. Why did they do that? They wanted to prevent Hindus or Sikhs from eating their grain. This was an unscrupulous and uncivilized act by those villagers. Was this taught in the Quran? No, it was pure stupidity, and no religion teaches such a thing. This was only a desperate act by these angry orthodox Muslims. Their minds were rotten, and they were acting against nature, but nature had something else in store for them. The whole village was camped near a small river on Grand Trunk Road between Phagwara and Jalandhar cantonment. They did what they could but had no control over nature. After two days of torrential rain, the river flooded and became the killer of the village; the entire Muslim camp was washed away. When the water subsided, people found dead bodies hanging on the broken trees with pockets full of gold and silver.

One day I happened to go to Dana Mandi Nakodar to buy sugar, masala, and some other items. There was a Hindu shop there, and the scene I witnessed was deplorable. It can never be effaced from my memory. I was appalled to think such insidious people existed in the world. The shop owner was selling lethal food grain (rotten corn with holes) to destitute, sick-looking Muslims. I knew about the Muslims' deep-seated aversion to Hindus, but this Hindu shop owner was inflicting real carnage. It was a heinous crime against humanity. These sadistic and hypocritical Hindu shopkeepers were dangerous to humankind and to the country. Although they worshipped their god's day and night, they lacked basic moral principles and acted like beasts. I hope God forgave them.

MY FATHER'S LOSSES
Unfortunately, in the leather business, our main customers were all Muslim shoemakers from Nakodar

and the surrounding villages. We had a pay-up system, and all the customers owed us a lot of money, around twenty thousand rupees. My father had no savings, and he put any surplus he had back into his business. There was no bank in Nakodar before 1947 except one Hindu cooperative bank, near Ram Mandir, but we never dreamed of going there due to the caste system. All the money my father had was tied up in the business, and we had no customers. What little money we had was lost now as all our customers were in camps and going to Pakistan, so overnight we became paupers. We had money tied up in leather processing and we had leather ready for sale, but our customers were gone.

As transportation and movement had come to a standstill, we were helpless. I remember how my mother heaved a sigh and asked my father what would happen now. My father laughed, but he was in a very bad mood. He answered that all his life he had worked honestly and diligently. His customers would eventually go to Pakistan, settle down, and then send the money. He firmly believed that earnings made honestly and with a lot of sweat would never go anywhere. But then he said to her, "You're moaning about your money, but look at their courage. They're leaving behind their forefathers' properties, homes worth millions of rupees. So, don't think about yourself; think about their fate, too." Then he said, "We made money from them, and if they took it, that's all right. Let's just pray for them to safely reach their destination." Such was my father's ethic of honesty, hard work, and belief in God.

We had three cows. My father never sold the milk to anyone but gave it freely to the villagers and needy ones. Now we were hard up ourselves, and my mother asked my father if he could sell the milk because she'd heard that a lot of people needed milk in the camp. But one day, two Sikhs came with daggers and took our animals by force. We were helpless to protect our belongings. At the same time, one of our workers came to the scene and told my father that his brother-in-law was visiting him and was in the military. My father asked the worker to bring the visitor in his uniform. My father sent three helpers with the military man and rescued our cows. Then we started to sell milk for the first time in our lives. My mother delivered the milk to our friends in the camp, they sold the milk, and in the evening, she collected the money from them. This was how we managed our household expenses until things returned to normal.

THE POLITICIANS' FOLLY

The partition was the result of hatred between Muslims and Hindus. Again, who would want to live in the society of Hindus, who believed in segregation and looked down on others whether they were Muslims, Sikhs, or untouchables? They refused to learn from their mistakes, and no one could teach them. Their metaphysical ideals had been destroying the unity of the country, and the country itself. It was high time they started to reconsider their insipid nature and what made them human beings worth being part of a fraternity.

I've wrestled with my conscience and agonized a great deal over the whole problem of the partition. Fifteen million humans moved to and from Pakistan. It was a terrible blunder, and over one million poor died during the move. Yet, ironically, every Hindu admired Mahatma Gandhi for his bloodless freedom. This perfectly demonstrates how people are sunk in ignorance. Those millions who died or suffered weren't Brahmans or mullahs or aristocrats; they were poor, illiterate, hardworking, good people and they had nothing to do with the partition. It was a tragedy. One could wonder if this murder of humanity was due to the shortage of good, passionate people in India who could have arranged a smooth migration without as much bloodshed. Or was its pure Brahmanism, belief in the orthodoxy of sacrifices to their spirits? Was it the egomania of Brahman and Muslim leaders that resulted in the murder of millions of innocent poor people? It hurt. Why didn't the leaders and politicians care? Those who died were not brothers or sisters or relatives of Jinnah and Nehru. This question of the mass murder's idiocy will haunt good people for many centuries to come. I wish this vicious crime hadn't happened, but it did.

After the partition, poor people lamented the cruelty of Muslim, Sikhs, and Hindus to the untouchables. They forgot that God had been watching the mistreatment the entire time and that the abusers would never be forgiven. Perhaps the calamity of the partition was due to sins these Muslims, Hindus, and Sikhs had committed in the past. Their sinful acts may have invited the wrath of God.

One thing was obvious: the departure of the Muslims from Punjab was a silver lining for the untouchables. It was God's gift to the millions of poor people because the Muslims were as bad as the Brahmans or Sikhs. They were full of prejudice and bigotry. Their departure was beneficial for the millions of untouchables who felt that it was better to suffer two evils than three. Many poor untouchables viewed the division of the country as a blessing in disguise because in Punjab, Muslims were the majority and quite powerful. They were as fanatical as the Brahmans. Their departure to Pakistan somehow reduced the burden of bigotry to some extent. Others saw it as a natural calamity to punish the Hindus, Sikhs, and Muslims for their crimes against humanity. The partition broke the Hindu, Muslim, and Sikh triangle in Punjab and gave the poor untouchables a chance to survive.

CHAPTER FOURTEEN

MOHAT RAM: MAN, OF GOODWILL AND ILL WILL

Mohat Ram was an Ayurvedic hakim who cured diseases using herbs and other curative natural products. He was soft-spoken, fair-skinned, and heavyset. He used to wear a turban on his shaven head, gold earrings, and a dhoti with a tunic and waistcoat. An experienced man of mature age, he knew the town of Nakodar and its surrounding villages. He was well known and respected in the town, as rich and poor people used to visit him for consultation and medicine. As a devout Brahman, he seemed to me entirely unconscious of morality and human values. He learned Ayurvedic practice and knowledge from his father and intended to pass on his valuable experience to his son.

He had two brothers: Sat Ram and Nant Ram. Sat Ram ran a shop next to Mohat Ram's place in the same building, in the heart of town. He used to sell juices, syrups, and ancillary products that Mohat Ram prescribed to his patients. Nant Ram ran his own iron and steel sales business. Like other Brahmans, they were also very caste-conscious and strongly believed in the caste system and segregation of untouchables, so they discriminated overtly.

SOCIAL SUFFERING

In the 1930s, my father was suffering from chronic bronchitis and needed medicine, so he chose to go to Mohat Ram when our family moved to Nakodar from an old village called Bhullar. Because my father was a leather maker, Mohat Ram and other high-caste Brahmans branded him as belonging to a low caste and didn't let him into the main hall where Mohat Ram sat and his high-caste friends surrounded him to ask for medicine and consultation. Instead, when my father or another family member went to Mohat Ram for medicine, they sat outside, in the front courtyard next to the street, on the cement floor. He used to treat my father by looking at the color of his urine sample, so every time we went for medicine, we carried a urine sample with us.

I was growing up and my father often told me to go to Mohat Ram for medicine. I had been to this place a few times with my father and never liked going there. However, this was an emergency, and other members of the family were busy working from early morning till late at night. At that time, my father couldn't afford to hire extra help to take a day off from his hard work. I was the only person left in the household who could go shopping and get medicine, which was two miles from home. Like my father, I had to sit in the front next to the main gate on a cement floor for hours. Sometimes I got soaked by the rain, and other times my loose turban was blown away by a storm. The wretched caste system didn't allow anyone to take pity on me, not even to let me take cover under a veranda. Worst of all, the high-caste customers used to take their shoes off and put them in front of me before going into the veranda or hall. I sat there like a chained stray dog among shoes for hours. This, to me, was an appalling crime against humanity. Inside my body I was burning with a certain kind of fire that no water could put out. There was nothing like a "first come, first served" rule. I was always the last one to get medicine thrown in the yard in front of me in small packets. Sometimes Mohat Ram forgot that I was sitting outside, and I had to send a message with someone to remind him. Those were the longest, most frustrating and bewildering days of my life. I still have these images in my mind.

After receiving the medicine and instructions on how to take it with syrup or other liquids, I went to the next shop, where his younger brother Sat Ram sold syrup. I used to put money on the cement floor in front of him. After pouring water over the money to purify it, he picked up the nickel piece and threw into the cash box. Why was all this necessary, I asked myself all the time. Why was I so humbled? Why was I always abused? I had a terrible sense of oppression all the time and I had to contain it for the sake of my father. There was a smoldering rage in my soul. This was just the way India was in the 1940s and before.

At times, tears gushed from my eyes. I felt totally helpless. My father sensed that I was hurt and grieved. I hated high-caste people. My uncle Lekh Chand complained to Mohat Ram for several years that I was a clean boy and getting educated but wasn't treated properly. Finally, Mohat Ram put a wooden bench there, which was a slight relief for me. I didn't have to sit on the ground, but I was still getting drenched in the rainy and stormy weather.

Mohat Ram had only a seventh-grade education, and I had reached the eighth grade. I was promoted to sit in the veranda on a bench, where he could see me easily from his seat on the carpeted floor with a big pillow behind his back in the big hall without getting up. After all those miserable years, my father and uncle met with him and he found us to be very gentle, honest, and civilized people. He became very friendly with my father and me. He started asking questions about my education and my family's welfare. He started speaking gently to me when we were alone. Sometimes he even visited my home when my father was very sick. My father was very humble, pleasant, and earnest toward Mohat Ram. Conditions between them changed greatly, but caste prejudice remained. Mohat Ram started showing affection to us and looked on us with loving eyes. Now I wasn't new to him and he was no stranger to me. I could go to him anytime, but mostly I started visiting in the afternoon, when he was alone or taking an afternoon nap in the hall. I sat on the bench, which was my proper place in the veranda. I waited until he awoke and then asked him for medicine.

MOHAT RAM'S DOZING CONSCIENCE

One afternoon, he awoke and saw me sitting on the bench in the veranda, reading my book. He called me in a loud but gentle voice to come and get the medicine from him. I didn't hear him and after a few minutes he called me again, but I was unsure of what he was saying. I asked him to repeat it. He wanted me to come into the hall and take the medicine from him. I couldn't believe my ears. He was asking me to enter and sit down. I was a little reluctant, but I did go in and sat four to five feet away from him. I wondered what caused his change in attitude toward me. It must have been that his dozing conscience compelled him to act this way, or maybe he was just too lazy to get up. I'd never had hope of being invited inside because this was an era of offense toward poor people. There was no one in the hall or in the veranda except him and me. He said that when he was alone in the hall, I could go in to get the medicine. At the same time, he told me he would lose his customers if he let me in while his other patients were there because most of them knew I was the son of an untouchable leather manufacturer. I felt a big wave of relief wash over me. God had come to help me.

MAN OF GOODWILL

He remained Brahman, but our friendship grew like anything. When he needed help, he always asked my father without hesitation. When we had any trouble, he was always there. We began to grow very close. As the hakim, he was affluent in the town. All the lawyers, police officers, and municipal officers used to come to him for medicine and consultation. On many occasions, he did his best to help us and spoke for us because he knew very well that we were humane, family-oriented people. After seventy-six years, I still remember and appreciate his help and thank him for everything he did for us. One time, some people filed a bogus case against my father stating that part of our big house was situated on their land and that we didn't consult them before building. They said we built the walls at nighttime to avoid talking to them. This was a serious matter for my father. First, he was a sick man, and second, he didn't want to create any ill feelings in the community. He asked well-known people in the community like Gurdet Singh, an MLA, to help solve the problem. My father told everybody that if the other party really believed he had occupied their land, which wasn't true, then he would give them an equal amount of land from all over the village. The other party agreed to the proposal one day but disagreed the next day. The mediators were irritated and gave up. Finally, Mohat Ram heard that the other party was causing problems for my father, who was a sick man and didn't want to be involved in civil cases. Mohat Ram, along with some other reputable townspeople, came to the village to mediate again and again, but the other party didn't budge. Finally, Mohat Ram told my father that he wouldn't have to worry about anything. Let them file the case in the court. Mohat Ram and his allies hired a lawyer friend and won easily. Then the other party appealed to a higher court and my father won again. After some time, the other party appealed the decision to the High Court and the case was thrown out.

In 1947, during the partition, everything was disrupted, and people had a hard time making a living. Some of my village's workers got day labor at the nearby railroad godown (warehouse), loading and unloading railroad wagons. Baksu Ram and Birk Ram, two brothers, were pushing a wagon to move it to the right place as instructed by the station authorities. They didn't know that some poor refugee kid was stealing grain from other wagons. When their wagon hit the other wagon, the child fell from the top of the wagon and died instantly. The police came and took the body of the deceased to the hospital. The workers were poor but good people. They were panicked and crying. The whole village was worried that the innocent workers would be jailed for a long time or hanged because the police and judges didn't listen to poor people. They rushed to my father. He was sick, but he sent a message to Mohat Ram about the serious situation. Mohat Ram intervened. He knew the police inspector and the case was dropped before it went to court. The whole family and my father still remember Mohat Ram for his act of kindness on behalf of the poor people.

Mohat Ram took good care of me. He was very happy and proud that I was going to college because his own family hadn't attended. I was preparing for my second-year final examination. Just a day before the exam, I felt sick. My throat began swelling and I could hardly talk. I rushed home in pain but couldn't explain what was happening to me. My father didn't know what to do. He listened to other orthodox people and called a village witch doctor in the middle of the night. I was very angry and told my father in writing that I was in a lot of pain and I would leave the house in the early morning to go to a hospital. My father sent my cousin early in the morning to explain my condition to Mohat Ram. He didn't believe that I was at home and sick. As far as he knew, I was sitting for the exam. He came at once and saw my poor condition. He was angry with my father for not informing him earlier or taking me to the hospital. Mohat Ram admitted me to the local hospital. Without his assistance, there was little chance of admittance as these doctors didn't care about the poor.

Before noon, they took me to the operating room, but the doctor in charge and his assistant couldn't find anything because of all the swelling. My mouth and neck were tight. They didn't know what to do. The doctor said to his assistant in English that they would operate on my throat, and if they couldn't find anything, they'd send me to the main hospital in Jalandhar. They didn't know I understood English. I tried to escape and pushed them away, but it was useless. They tied me to the bed and soon they heard a car horn. The doctor rushed outside to welcome the doctor from Jalandhar Main hospital. He came into the operating room and examined me. He told the doctor to open my mouth and pull one of my bad teeth. As soon as the tooth was pulled, blood started gushing out and the swelling started going down. I spent a week in the hospital, and I was saved.

There were many other instances when Mohat Ram came in good stead. He was a devout Brahman, so he never touched us, and we didn't touch him, but our hearts were one and touching. My father spent hours discussing our family problems with him and listening to his family problems. My father proved a big asset to him, and Mohat Ram was never a liability to us. Some of his Brahman friends didn't like my father going inside the hall, and I overheard Mohat Ram telling some of his orthodox friends that my father had more humanity in his little finger than they had in their entire bodies.

His brother Sat Ram was full of prejudice, too. He used to keep a separate cup for us if we wanted to drink water or syrup. He pointed to the cup on the dirty shelf near the street edge. Sometimes, old dead bees and mosquitoes were in it and it was hard to clean even after two or three washes. He used to pour water in the tumbler from two feet high. After drinking, we had to put it back in the same place. This was the custom among orthodox Brahmans in the 1930s, but by the time I finished high school and went to college, these customs had begun to crumble. Sat Ram's son happened to become acquainted with me during the school external examination and later became a friend. I used to meet him in the shop for a drink on my way home. He was very ashamed of his father's behavior when I pointed out that his father made me drink water from that dirty cup on the dirty shelf near the street.

When he decided to go abroad and asked me to join him, I was in trouble as I was married and not earning anything, and wasn't doing well in my studies, either. I hoped to get a BA and then take a government job as a clerk, like many others. But when I learned what the monthly salary would be, I nearly fainted. He told me how and where to apply for a passport before he left for England. So, it was Mohat Ram's nephew who gave me a lead and advice to apply for my passport and get out of the country if I wanted a better life. He died after reaching Scotland and I always remember him and thank him for his good advice. Mohat Ram was very proud of my father and I and felt that we were good in every respect, but we never shook hands or touched each other. It shows that things were much better than before, but caste problems were still far from solved. This was India in the 1940s and before.

CHAPTER FIFTEEN

MY COLLEGE YEARS

I hadn't wanted to attend college because of the very poor marks I earned on my high school exam. I wasn't sure if any college would admit me. My relative Shiv Raj insisted that I try to get admitted. However, I went to Jalandhar, and on the road, I met MLA Gurdet Singh, a friend of my father. He took me to his office, and I happened to mention that I had passed high school. He told me I must attend college, but before I could explain further, he gave me a note for the principal and asked me to go to DAV (Dayanand Anglo Vedic) College. With that note from Gurdet Singh, I was admitted to college in Jalandhar.

It was a very exciting day for me as I had never been to any college. I felt elated at being a college student. I was very anxious to see the campus. I soon met an old peon and asked him to show me around if he was available. The college was situated on the famous Grand Trunk Road to Amritsar, about two miles from the city center at a railroad crossing. It had two gates on the main part of Grand Trunk Road. The college consisted of many red brick buildings and verandas and big green lawns spread over a distance. I was so pleased to see the Lajpat Rai Library at the college. It was housed in a separate building. Next, I saw the science block, another building filled with laboratories. When I stepped into the administrative building hall, I felt as if I was in a magnificent palace. Many rooms were attached to the halls used for holding classes. Students were dressed in European styles and seemed quite comfortable in them.

I was late entering college and the hostel on the opposite side of the campus was full. I was married, and my wife was staying with my parents. I tried to travel by train, but it wasn't easy because the station was far from the college. After a few weeks, I started staying with an old couple in a nearby village called Ram Nagar. That place wasn't suitable to me at all since I didn't want to be a burden to an old couple. I'd never been all on my own, and I felt very lonely and homesick.

During the weekends, I visited my parents and my wife. Soon my father bought a new bicycle for me to ride back and forth to Nakodar on weekends and to college. I loved walking the short distance to college and sometimes, when it was raining, other students offered me a lift and I took it. They became friendly to me. There was no question of caste as no one knew each other and most students were refugees from Pakistan. I used to dress in well pressed clothes.

One day I took my bicycle to college and it started raining. At the end of the day, some boys were waiting for the bus and they saw me with a bike and stopped me. I couldn't refuse them, so I offered to take one of them with me. They took the bike from me and put me in the front and started pedaling. There were three of them, and a policeman at the crossing tried to stop us, but the boys didn't stop. Then another policeman tried to stop us, and we were caught and taken to the police station. The other boys were joking with each other, but I was trembling in fear of the police. The police asked for their fathers' names and addresses, and to my surprise, one of the boys was the son of a police officer and another one was the son of a doctor. Before they had even filled out the forms, we were freed. After this incident, I never rode my bike to college again.

My first impression of college life was very interesting. It presented an altogether different picture from school life. The rules and regulations of the college weren't strict, and the students were fined for breaches of discipline and misbehavior. There was plenty of freedom and no caste discrimination. The professor went on lecturing without even caring whether the students followed the lecture or not.

DOMESTIC PROBLEMS

But soon, my interest in college started to wear off because of my domestic problems. First, I had no good place to live and I was unable to study at my residence. Second, my wife was suffering with her eyes. That worried me a lot and kept me from concentrating on my studies. I started taking the day off from college whenever she had appointments at the Ludhiana eye hospital. It was a challenging situation whether I stayed at college and let her go blind or take her to the hospital. The third reason was that I wasn't working. I was dependent on my parents to study and live, and some family members had a problem with our dependency. I was given about thirty-five rupees per month to spend, which wasn't much at all. My father always wanted to know where I spent the money and I had to keep records of every penny I spent. I had no friends, so I was always homesick and sometimes I wanted to watch movies. One incident that happened was when Shenker Dutt asked me whether I had seen any movies or not. Without thinking, I narrated the story of the movie I had seen to him while we were sitting alone near the fireplace in the evening. He went to my father and told him I'd been going to the movies. My father called me to his bedside and admonished me that he didn't give me money to see movies. Movies were a waste of money and time for him because he'd never been to the movies in his life. I was in tears and didn't sleep all night. The next morning, I left early for the bus station without picking up my weekly ration of atta and dal (wheat flour and dry pulse). I ended up missing the earlier bus, but before I caught the second bus that ran an hour or two later, I saw my mother carrying my stuff to the bus station. I felt bad for causing her trouble and we both went home. Life turned very miserable for me, like a bed of thorns, and I still remember the hardships and agonizing days of college life. I call this period the "dark days" of my life.

From that day on, I stopped telling my brother anything, but my father still wanted the record of my spending every month. The price of a third-class movie ticket was seven annas in those days, and a glass of milk also cost seven annas, so I started writing that I drank a glass of milk instead of going to a movie now and then. I wasn't happy to tell even little white lies, but there was no other way because I was barred from going to the movies. Every month my father remarked that I was drinking enough milk but not getting fat as I was underweight and slim.

I didn't like arguments about small matters in the

house. I was very sensitive, so I told my wife to go to her mother's and stay there until I could finish my studies and find work. I started going to my in-laws' every week against the advice of my father.

THE HINDU CODE BILL

While I was at college, some other major events took place. From the college notice board, I learned about a debate on the Hindu Code Bill at the local women's college. This topic was the subject of interesting discussions and debates all over India. In Jalandhar, I attended two debates between young women from Kanya Maha Vidyalaya (the only women's college in Jalandhar at that time) and some old orthodox Hindus who were against Dr. Ambedkar and his bills. A young Hindu woman gave compelling examples, questioning why she had to wait till midnight to eat dinner with her drunken, cruel old husband. Why had her parents married her to this man in the first place? Another girl argued against the dowry system, saying that a poor man couldn't afford a dowry and their daughters were forced to marry rotten old men. The old orthodox men cried that the Hindu religion was in danger and the bill was against their holy books. In 1951 and before, there was a lot of illiteracy, and resolutions were passed against the bill. Even the Hindu president of India, Dr. Rajinder Parshad, and other leaders like Sardar Patel opposed it. They were unwilling to free the women from their clutches. The Hindu Code Bill was dead. It couldn't pass. Dr. Ambedkar was so utterly frustrated that in September 1951 he resigned from his post as law minister.

He started preparing for the 1952 general election. He came to Jalandhar Boota Mandi as part of his election campaign and gave an impressive and illuminating speech. My father had business friends there, and with their help, I managed to get close enough to listen and enjoy his speech. I consider myself lucky to have had the honor and privilege to listen to his talk. The next day, the DAV college authorities invited him to visit. He met the students of my community in Lajpat Rai Library. There were fewer than a dozen students at the college then. I had the good fortune of standing there with Dr. Ambedkar. He asked only one simple question: what we were studying? Some students said arts and others answered non-medical. He said very gently that he was less concerned with what we studied and more that whatever we studied, we would finish it completely and have a thorough knowledge of the subject. It was a great moment. I still remember his words and they served me as an inspiration and advice, a most cherished possession. The principal was absent that day, but Dr. Ambedkar had a photograph taken with the college staff and it hung in the principal's office afterward.

Dr. Ambedkar dedicated his life to the betterment and uplifting of the millions of untouchables and downtrodden in India. He was born to an untouchable family, and like millions of others, he was the victim of caste prejudice and discrimination by orthodox Indian society. After finishing his studies in India, he continued in America with the help of the Maharaja of Baroda. He studied law at Columbia University in New York, earning MAs in 1915 and 1916. In 1921, he earned an MSc. His thesis *The Problem of the Rupee* earned him his Doctor of Science degree in 1923, and then he passed the barrister exam and became a barrister. In April 1923, he returned to India as B. R. Ambedkar, DSc, MA, MSc, Bar-at-law. Later, in 1927, he earned his PhD in economics. Despite all his education in India, America, and England, he was still tormented by orthodox Hindus who didn't consider him a human being.

On August 15, 1947, India became a free country and Jawaharlal Nehru became the prime minister. Nehru liked Dr. Ambedkar and persuaded him to join the cabinet, so he was soon sworn in as a law minister. The first thing independent India needed was a constitution, and Dr. Ambedkar was made chairman of the constitution-drafting committee at Nehru's suggestion. On November 26, 1948, the draft constitution presented by Dr. Ambedkar was passed and it became the constitution of independent India, a legal instrument of the nation.

On June 5, 1952, Columbia University in New York conferred on Dr. Ambedkar the honorary degree of Doctor of Law. Soon after the passage of the constitution, Dr. Ambedkar introduced the Hindu code bills to the parliament. The aim of the bills was to remove the oppressive customs and traditions of Hindu society. The bills raised a hue and cry among old orthodox Hindus all over India, and the leaders who praised Ambedkar for his work on the constitution turned against him, except for Prime Minister Nehru.

One day I learned Mahatma Gandhi was coming to Ludhiana, Punjab. I wanted to see this great man and went to Ludhiana, but the train ran late, and I missed him. I was very disappointed. A few months later, Prime Minister Nehru came to Punjab regarding the general elections. He stopped at the old fort in Phillaur. I first saw him from a distance. He was up on the platform in front of the old fort, the concluding speaker at the 1952 election. I was below in the vast crowd of listeners on the other side of the deep trench. That day I saw the real Jawaharlal Nehru, the one I'd never dreamed of. His motorcade was late, and the large crowd was frustrated and noisy. One congressman declared over the loudspeaker that Panditji, as India called Nehru, was getting angry, and therefore they needed to keep quiet. Nehru turned so angry after hearing the announcement that he shook the man violently and nearly threw him off the platform. After his speech, he wanted to return to the motorcade. The crowd was so unorganized and dense, he heard policemen cursing at the public to clear his path through the crowd. At one point, he snatched the stick from a policeman and made his own way through the unruly crowd.

I completed two years in college, but only days before the final examination, I fell sick. My whole mouth was swollen, and I had to go home and was admitted into the hospital for a week. After that I stayed in Jalandhar but didn't attend college. My parents believed I was still in college. I stayed with my sister's husband in Boota Mandi and applied for a passport, but I didn't tell my parents I had done so. When I needed money, I asked my sister's husband and he was reimbursed by my parents with no questions asked. So, after spending two years in college, I didn't pass my examination. Nonetheless, I'd gained enough knowledge to stand on my own feet. I learned a sense of responsibility that I couldn't escape, paying full attention to my wife's illness and not caring much about my studies. The true aim of a college education is to enlarge the mind and learn to grasp things in one's own way. I learned those lessons well, so the two years weren't wasted.

CHAPTER SIXTEEN

A DREADFUL NIGHT

It was the fall of 1952 and my father was a very busy person as he had to do all sorts of things to keep the household together. During this time, he decided to arrange the marriage of my niece. This engagement had been set a few years earlier. My father consulted my mother and older brother and fixed the date of the ceremony before the cold weather set in. He had a big problem on his hands with inviting the guests on such short notice. At twenty-one years old, my father gave me the responsibility to invite his relatives and friends from far and near. I was the only credible person in the family, as well as in the neighborhood, at that time who could read and write and ride a bicycle to get around.

The date of the marriage was drawing near, and my father's mind was focused on my progress. I had my own problems and was steeped in worries as some relatives were living in far remote villages. I wasn't sure if they would get their invitations in time because of the poor mail system.

One important relative was from a village called Deowal. One Sunday night, my father suggested that I go there myself and invite them. I had no clue where that small village was or how to get there. I inquired of my father and some other people. The village was far from the railroad track and required walking a few miles after getting off the train. There were no cars or taxis in the villages in those days. The only option left for me was to go by bicycle. I wasn't keen on going to these relatives because I didn't know them, except for their elders.

The monsoon weather was just ending and lots of water had gathered in the lowlands, so the foot paths were not good to travel. However, I didn't want to refuse as it was a matter of honor for the family to invite them on my family's behalf. Thus, it was inevitable that I would agree with my father and brother. I took my bicycle in the early morning and checked the tires. My mother quickly made me breakfast and I rode to Deowal, following the winding dirt roads from village to village. I asked for directions to the sweets shop and brought sweets as my father had firmly instructed me not to arrive emptyhanded.

It took me about two hours to get to my destination as the wind was pushing me faster. Finally, I managed to get to the right house after stopping here and there in the villages inquiring about the family's whereabouts. Since the house had no numbers on it, I had to verify which house it was by the name of the relative.

AN OLD, BACKWARD VILLAGE

These people were thrilled to see me. The crowded house was overflowing with innocent and beautiful children, just sitting there passing the time, and I had lunch with them. It immediately struck me that the whole household consisted of farm workers who were half starved, and it seemed like they were working for a meager handful of wheat. They looked very depressed. They were very humble and respectful and had peculiar habits, like spitting here and there or cleaning their noses in the presence of another person. I didn't like these mannerisms at all. I didn't know all the members of the family. One young boy showed a special interest and respect for me. He must have learned about me from his parents.

In the evening, after giving them the invitation, I said goodbye to the family. The young boy, who was named Prem, wanted to go out to his job. He begged me to stay overnight as he found me interesting and wanted to know more about me, but I kept telling him I couldn't stay overnight and fabricated a story that made it sound as though it was urgent for me to go home that evening. Outside, the fires of a blazing sun started to go down in the western horizon and I asked for my bicycle.

Beru Ram, the big brother, nodded his head and brought me my bicycle. To my surprise, it was in very poor condition. The front tire was flat, the tire and tube were cut with a sharp knife. I was boiling with rage, yet I couldn't show it. Beru Ram told me that his brother Prem was angry with me for not staying, so he must have cut the tube. Beru Ram told me to stay overnight and leave early in the morning. He said he would get the bicycle repaired, but I was more adamant than ever to leave that evening. I was running out of time.

Beru Ram couldn't find any repairman in the neighborhood; he had a vague recollection that someone repaired bicycles in a nearby village. He walked with me there. The repairman was a carpenter by profession but did other small jobs to earn extra money. He repaired the tire and tube of the bicycle, but by the time he finished, it was pitch dark. All I could see were the kerosene lamps in the village shops. Beru was worried and cajoled me to turn back to his house.

TRAVELING IN THE DARK

I said goodbye to him, but he wasn't happy. Before I left the village, I asked an older person about the distance of the railroad track to Nakodar, my town. He told me where the shortcuts were and that the distance was about twelve miles. I became a little scared because of the darkness, but then I wondered who would see or meet me in the darkness anyway. I took my small knife from my bicycle pouch and put it in my front pocket. I also found a small, strong stick and started bicycling. I kept my eyes on the white, creamy, dirt road that was barely visible. In a few minutes, I turned onto a dingy footpath and headed toward the desolate fields.

After some time, I heard someone shouting and a dog barking. I was going in their direction. The man was standing with a big stick in front of me. I told him I was lost and wanted to go to Shankar, a small town near the railroad track. I also mentioned to him that I was the relative of a local MLA, which was a big lie. I was afraid he would take a harsh attitude toward me. The man told me to go back about half a mile and then take a right turn. I was fighting against time, but it was inky dark, and I was unable to see much of anything. All I knew was that I was in the agricultural fields. I wasn't sure whether I was going north or south. Everything looked the same in the thick darkness.

Then, after traveling a mile or so, I started hearing

a grinding machine noise. This was somehow an indication that I was going in the right direction. I was thinking about this, and suddenly I found my front wheel in a small ditch. I jumped off the bicycle. There was no footpath; the field was plowed for new crops. It was a big puzzle to me. There was no sense carrying the bicycle on my shoulder and plodding through the field to find the footpath on the other side. All I was sure about was that I would find the footpath because the plowed field wasn't very big.

Instead of carrying the bicycle with me, I left it at one corner of the field and trudged across, looking for the footpath. After some time, I found it, but then I lost my bicycle. A lot of time and sweat was wasted looking for both the bicycle and the footpath. After a hard struggle, I managed to get out of the dark jungle. I was baffled, bored and late, and worried that my father would be unhappy with me for traveling so late. As I peddled along, the footpath grew a little better and wider, and I knew I was approaching another village because I could see white graves (*matti*) here and there. These white graves tricked my mind, and suddenly I was struck on the head with something and fell to the ground. I was immediately possessed by a tidal wave of fear and panic. Silently I asked the Almighty to give me strength to endure whatever was to come. I rummaged and tried to look around but didn't see anything. My heart was beating wildly, and I could hardly breathe. I was in shock. It was terrifying. I picked up my bicycle and set the front wheel straight. I stood there for a while where I had landed, looking around with an open knife in my hand. I checked my knees and legs for injuries; one knee was slightly bruised, but it was all right.

I eventually walked along on foot for a couple of minutes and I was feeling and walking all right. There was nobody around because it was so dark. Then, I asked myself who attacked me and how I fell from the bicycle. There had to be something or somebody that made me fell. The conflict in my soul was not over. I turned around and went back to where I fell. This time I was on foot and was gently struck again. I discovered that it was a Banyan tree with big, rough roots hanging down from the main trunk. These roots were thick because it was a very old tree. After a sigh of relief, I drove the bicycle further and reached the railroad track. I felt a slight wave of relief wash over me.

Now I was sure to get home without any further trouble. All I had to do was follow the track. But it wasn't easy, as the many stones made riding the bicycle challenging. Occasionally, a small tree in a nearby field looked like a man waiting for me, but I had enough courage to face any kind of problem.

Finally, I reached home as midnight approached after a long and exhausting journey. My mother was awake and smoking quietly. She was waiting for me and was worried. The other family members, including my father, were sleeping. I lifted my bicycle onto my shoulder and took my shoes off without making any noise. After seeing that I had arrived home safely, my mother was happy and gave me food to eat. I begged her not to tell my father and the others about my late arrival. I promised her I would never travel so late again and withdrew into my room. At last, I was happy to get out of this predicament.

CHAPTER SEVENTEEN

RELIGION

My parents were very religious; they had their own personal set of religious beliefs. Religion is a personal thing and they did whatever comforted them and gave them inner peace. Sometimes I understood their actions, but other times I didn't. On the very first day of every month, my father made a lot of sweet pudding and distributed it among the village children, or my mother made sweet rice and invited a lot of young girls to have a good feast in our house. Before eating, my mother or father always lit candles or oil candles and performed rituals, praying to remember their ancestors and ask for their blessings. They believed that the holy spirit of their forefathers would protect the family and help them in everyday life.

On some auspicious occasions, my mother was always accompanied by some children to a bush in a faraway field where a snake was supposed to live. She lit the candle, said a prayer for blessings, and distributed sweets to the children. I didn't like snakes, and I always refrained from going along with my mother to the bushes. Every day, early in the morning, my father would recite some holy part of the Gurbani. He remembered all of it by heart and recited it with amazing speed, but nobody could understand what he was saying. Then, sometimes, he brought home some wandering sadhus, fed them, gave them a small tip (gift), and asked for their blessings. My father found comfort in feeding and helping sadhus. He never forgot to pay respect to the graves of Muslim peers.

Our village was very small and had no gurdwara or mandir. There were no gurdwaras in the surrounding villages. There was a Hindu Ram mandir in the town, but we weren't allowed to go inside because the Hindus observed the caste system. To save ourselves from humiliation, we never tried to go to the gurdwara or mandir. Instead my father bought a big volume of the holy book called *Guru Nanak Ki Sakhi*. At times of celebration, he read for a few hours every day and finished in so many days. After a year or so, he bought *Valmiki Ramayana* and the Mahabharata, and then he bought Guru Ravidass Deep. He read all the religious books time and time again. He brought some knowledgeable sadhus into the house to discuss important topics in these books. My father had more knowledge about the books than most of the Brahman lords of the religion. When I was young, I oversaw the care of the books. My father often bought beautiful cloth pieces and asked me to wrap them and put them in a safe place with care. I always listened to these readings with great interest.

As the years passed, I turned from stereotype to rationalism. I became very inquisitive and stopped believing in mysticism. I stopped believing in a blind faith. I stopped going to religious places where all men of God weren't treated equally. I never attended any Hindu mandir and communion after the days of my childhood, when a priest threw stones at me and hurt my leg. Even in the gurdwara I didn't find real comfort because of segregation and caste beliefs. I didn't believe in any other manmade cults or organizations made to rob illiterate and innocent people.

A TRUE RELIGION

Up to now, these religions and cults have done more harm than good to their countries. They have divided countries and killed millions of innocent and poor people. I think I can do without such religions and cults, which spread and preach nothing but hatred against each other. The whole world is in turmoil and that is ample proof of the value of religion or religious life.

A true religious person is one who believes in the common good, helps their neighbors and the needy, tells the truth, and is kind to their surroundings no matter which faith they belong to. God is everywhere; God doesn't live in mandirs or gurdwaras or masjids. God is not the property of Brahmans, maulvis, or *preachers*. God is within you, and if you're serving the community, the brotherhood of man, you're serving God. I didn't find any solace in any religion. I wish the world knew better.

Keeping myself away from religious places doesn't make me nonreligious or atheist. My God is within me all the time. My God stops me from doing or thinking bad things. I'm afraid of God and I can't escape from Him because He is within me and watching over me all the time. You can call it whatever you want, you can call it *atma*, consciousness, but without *atma* or fear of God, we're just like beasts, or even worse.

My uncle entered my religion in the school registration as Hindu, but ever since I met a Hindu priest, I've never felt good about Hinduism. I don't know much about Hinduism, except for its interesting epic stories that sometimes don't make sense. I'm not proud to be called Hindu as it has too many fundamentalist flaws in it. I respect all religions because religions themselves aren't bad, but people who preach religion and make a mockery of it are. These evil brutes have destroyed humanity, the brotherhood of men of the same soil. These fanatics don't know the real meaning of religion. They take it like opium and talk nonsense, proving themselves a curse to society. Opportunists exploit religion for their own interests, and politicians use religion as their vote bank. It's tragic that the misuse of religion has become the culture of the notorious.

Religion, instead of bringing goodwill among communities, has introduced poison into everyday life. Religion has brought about communal riots and upheaval in countries and has proved a curse to mankind. The rich and mighty, the most powerful and naughty, have made religion a standing joke. One should believe more in morality and ethics than in religious doctrine. Love and respect for the country should be given preference over all types of religions. If a country like India wants to survive, it shouldn't mix religion with politics and should keep orthodox communal groups like Brahmans, mullahs and *preachers*, the notorious lords of religion, away from governing the country.

CHAPTER EIGHTEEN

PRIDE & PREJUDICE

Discrimination under the caste system persisted throughout my life in India. In this chapter, I offer a collection of stories about my experiences with this ill-treatment and hypocrisy. The caste or untouchability is not written on one's face. It is all subjective and arbitrary. It is a question of one's mind and makeup. One should be proud of what he or she is. There is no real question of caste and creed, but some ignorant people have made it a big issue for their own advantage.

THE WHEAT FARMER

I remember a trip to meet a wheat farmer. Mohat Ram, our Brahman hakim friend, sent a message to my father that he'd bought three loads of straw (*turi*), animal feed, at a low price, one for himself and two for us from his patient, who was a Jat Sikh farmer. During the week, his son had gone to the farmer and brought home one load, and for the other two loads, I had to go to the farmer's village. On the weekend, I was home from college and my father gave me instructions and the farmer's address. The old farmer and his sons met me in the fields and comforted me on a charpoy (a movable bed) with beautiful new sheet and pillow under a shady tree in the hot summer weather. While they were busy weighing and loading the carts, I was sitting and writing all the weights on a clean piece of paper. They treated me nicely, giving me ice cold water and fresh cucumber from the field.

When all the weighing was completed and the two carts were loaded, we proceeded to my village. After crossing the town, the farmer asked me where we were going. I told him to turn right after the railroad crossing. After turning right, the farmer became very inquisitive and asked me what caste I belonged to. He thought I was a Brahman boy because he'd sold the loads to a Brahman. He never asked me about caste and I never told him, otherwise he would have treated me differently. From then on, he was not in a good mood and didn't talk to me.

However, he unloaded the two carts and my father gave him the money he brought, new notes from the bank. To be nice to the farmer, my father asked him what else he could do for him. The farmer replied in a grim voice that the money was all right, but I had polluted all his clothes and utensils. My father had more notes in his hand and immediately gave some to the farmer. He told him to throw the bedclothes and utensils away and buy new ones.

The farmer was happy and accepted the money but insisted that I should have told him my caste before touching the utensils. My father told him I was clean, a college student, and didn't believe in the caste system like he and they did. The farmer gave me a hard look, then muttered a curse and walked away. Like this farmer, a lot of astonishingly ignorant people out there still haven't abolished untouchability from their hearts.

One summer day when I was in high school, my father asked me to bring some fodder from the field for the animals. As I went to get it, one of my distant cousins who was working saw me and without telling anybody, he came to greet me. Soon the young farmer boy came after him and started swearing at him and insulting him. I couldn't tolerate his dirty words. I had a newspaper in my hand, and I hit him with it. He was younger than me. I don't know why his face started bleeding; maybe he already had a scratch on it.

Suddenly, everyone cutting the wheat joined him, including his father. I told the father that his son had used bad language and I couldn't tolerate it. I asked him why, if I'd used the same inappropriate language, he wouldn't tolerate it, but nobody listened to me. Instead, they took me to his well. I thought they were going to beat me. In the meantime, my distant uncle appeared there. He begged them with folded hands to let me go as I was a nice person. They didn't want me to go. They decided to put me in the well. Some talked about lynching me. I told my uncle to go to Mohat Ram and tell him I couldn't see him because I was in trouble here. Then I mentioned the name of a police inspector who was my friend and told him to explain what was happening here. Hearing the names of Mohat Ram and the police inspector, the farmers got scared.

Some of them changed their minds because they went to Mohat Ram for medicine. Finally, they let me go. They didn't ask the boy why he was using dirty language, but they wanted to beat me. It was precisely the collision of immoral power and dictatorship with powerless morality that constituted a crisis.

THE CROOKED POLICEMAN

I used to buy stationery and pens from Guru Ram Faquir Chand, a well-established shop in Bansawala Bazaar in Nakodar. It was a convenient shop and the shopkeeper knew me. I wanted a better pen than what he showed me.

Suddenly a stranger appeared there on his bike. He was taller and older than me, he had no long hair, no turban and a fancy cut beard and mustache. He looked like a goonda (goon). He interrupted while I was joking with the shopkeeper, saying I would get the good pen at the police station. There was something sinister in his voice.

"There are plenty of people like you there, and they won't mind another one," I retorted.

The shopkeeper was annoyed and told him to keep quiet and let me buy the pen.

I left the shop on my bike and noticed him following me. I had a long trip home through desolate fields, and I was afraid he was following me to cause trouble. I knew the town streets very well and made lot of twists and turns to get rid of him, but he persisted. Finally, I made a sharp turn and hid behind the big door of a friend's shop. He roamed around in the streets for a few minutes, and my friend asked him if he'd lost something. He said he'd lost a chicken and walked away. Then I was able to go home. The next day I learned he was a peon at the local thana (police station) and a Jat Sikh. He told my friend that I hadn't saluted them when he and the police inspector passed me near my village. He wanted to teach me how to salute police.

THE EYE HOSPITAL

Nasib Kaur was admitted to the eye hospital in Ludhiana and there was no provision for food. It was too difficult and tedious to bring food from home every day, so we decided to cook food on the big lawn of the hospital, where many other patients were cooking. One day, in my absence, a Jat Sikh village woman, a patient, asked my wife to lend her a pan for a short time. My wife was alone and afraid of getting into trouble in a new place. She told the woman that she belonged to the chamar community, and if she didn't mind that, then she could use a pan. After hearing this, the village woman started shouting, "Why you are lying at this young age about a minor thing? Don't give me your pan, but don't lie about it!"

Nasib Kaur was in tears, and soon I appeared there, and she told me everything. I told the woman that my wife was telling the truth and to prevent further trouble, I bought a new pan for her. This woman thought my wife was lying about belonging to the chamar community because she was a neat and clean person, more so than the woman was. These high-caste ignorant people always thought the chamar community was filled with dirty-looking people, and like their elders, they looked down on us and didn't expect us to wear clean clothes.

THE WELL

It was a Saturday evening, all our relatives and friends had gone home, and the marriage ceremony had ended with great pomp. My father told me to return the bedsheets, blankets, and beds (charpoys) and other things I'd borrowed from friends in a distant village called Ludher. In those days it was customary for friends and neighbors to help as much as they could with wedding or other social gatherings.

I hired a bullock cart with two drivers, then loaded it with beds, sheets and blankets and left for Ludher the next morning. The village was six miles away and I had to follow a sandy track. For a mile or so I walked behind the cart. I felt tired and decided to climb up and sit on the beds. The cart kept moving slowly along the sandy path and I was sitting in the scorching heat of the sun and sweating. I was very thirsty and saw a farm well far away on the trail. When we reached it, I asked the driver to stop the cart and I got off. An old Sikh farmer was watering his fields and I asked his permission to drink from the well. He replied in the affirmative. I leaned down, put one hand in the open square pipe and drank the flowing water. The cart drivers were thirsty too, so they did the same.

When the old man saw them drinking the water, he burned up with rage and started screaming. "You fools don't know the difference between a cow and a donkey (between good and the bad)! Why are you polluting my well and water?" He tried to hit them with the long stick in his hand.

I was shocked at the old man's behavior. I stopped him and tried to explain that I'd asked for his permission to drink the water. He wasn't listening to me and repeated the same words again and again, that they'd polluted his well.

I told the drivers to move away and drive the cart to the village before we had any more problems. Both drivers were strong, workers in the grain market, lifting heavy loads in the open air and their skin was dark, burned by the intense heat of the sun. However, we quenched our thirst and were feeling good when we reached the village.

I met my friends and narrated the whole episode to them. They told me that old farmer was a superstitious troublemaker and I did right by getting away from him. I gave the beds to the owners and thanked them. On our return journey, we had to cross the same well on the same path. There was no other way. We saw from a distance that three men were standing and blocking the path. We expected trouble. I told the drivers to let me talk first and tell them the truth. But the drivers were more worried for their lives than I was and expected grave danger. They stopped and took two special sticks fitted with spears from their hidden pouch in the cart.

As we drew near the well, the farmers growled at us, "How dare you! You've insulted our old father and polluted the well because he was old and alone."

I earnestly told them that we respected their father and had not insulted him. I had asked him for water and he gladly gave me permission to drink water from the well. There was no question of insult. But they wanted to fight and teach the drivers a lesson for polluting their well.

They called the drivers untouchables and repeated that they had polluted the well. Then I interrupted, saying that they were my elder brothers. I attended college and didn't work outside in the burning heat of the sun, I claimed. I had good clean clothes on, and my skin color was a lot lighter than that of the drivers and farmers. Because of my clothes, they thought I was a Brahman or another higher caste member.

In the meantime, the indignant drivers could bear no more of the farmers' insults and dirty language. They couldn't conceal their emotions and they challenged the farmers to a fight. When the farmers saw the spears, they cooled down and walked away. Finally, we reached home safely, and I narrated the whole story to my father, who blamed me more than the farmers. Such was his depressed soul and nature, always favoring others.

THE HORSE
Nasib Kaur and I were visiting my sister about five or six miles from Phillaur and missed the early morning train returning to Nakodar. The next train was later in the evening. My wife insisted that instead of waiting in Phillaur for the next train, we should walk. I wasn't ready for that, but she kept pushing me to walk. We followed the railroad track on foot and passed the Nurmahal station, but then she got tired and we missed the evening train. As we approached the Sidhwan train station, we saw an old farmer running and shouting at us. We thought he wanted to ask us something, so we stopped. The man thought my wife was pregnant. He offered his horse to ride and we thanked him. This was another form of good people. My wife was very impressed, and I told her that he offered a ride because he didn't know what caste we belong to. Otherwise he would have blamed us for polluting his horse, and even more probably, never would have offered a ride, but he had done so and we were thankful to him wholeheartedly.

THE PRIEST
Although I was short and weak as a child, I became ever more naughty and stubborn as I grew older. I was getting used to punishments and warnings from my

father and teachers. I never accepted it when teachers or others told me I was inferior to them, and I believed in my heart they were wrong. I was a very angry boy and often touched the high-caste boys deliberately despite warnings from the teacher. I wasn't afraid of my teachers.

In fourth grade, my distant cousin and I happened to meet an old Brahman priest while walking to the train station. He was naked save a white loincloth, with a tuft of hair on the top of his shaven head and a sacred thread hanging from his shoulder to his waist. He had red, burning, frightening eyes. He used to walk on a sandy track from town to a train station to catch an early train and we met him every day through the week. He looked at us with anger in a provocative way every time. My father told me to leave the track and let him pass as the Brahman priests expected us to. I was determined not to leave the track, and instead made the Brahman step off. Anytime I looked at him he was murmuring something, perhaps cursing us, and his behavior made me angry. I copied him and started murmuring too. This encouraged me to defy the old bad habits at an early age, and sometimes I enjoyed this kind of mischief, which my father and others did not expect of me.

HYPOCRISY

I'm just a simple person who believes in liberty and justice for all. When I was in school in Punjab, I suffered a lot because of caste prejudice. We avoided the gurdwaras because of the humiliation and insults. Instead, my father bought a holy book called *Guru Nanak ki Sakhi* and read it on auspicious occasions such as the birthday of Guru Nanak Dev Ji. I listened to

Bani with great interest and gained more knowledge by reading and listening to other scriptures.

Guru Nanak was the founder of Sikhism and I truly believe he denounced caste, untouchability, and segregation, something Hindu Brahmans practiced and preached all the time. I experienced the same caste-related problems with some orthodox Jat Sikhs in the villages. They looked down on me although, as a human being, I was better than them in many ways. They were rude and ill-mannered. They hurled filthy abuses and were rotten to the core. They created an atmosphere of fear and coercion. They were power-corrupt. There was fierce repression and suppression of all kinds. I felt very uncomfortable whenever I met them. To me they were not good Sikhs because they never followed the good teachings of Guru Nanak, and that has troubled me profoundly. His teachings denounced the caste system and taught that everyone was equal regardless of caste. He spoke of the universal love of humility, brotherhood, equality, fraternity, and virtue. In my experience, not many Sikhs follow his teachings, yet ironically they are proud to call themselves his followers. In 1940 and earlier in the villages, poor untouchables were only allowed to do farm work. The Jat Sikhs and other farmers paid the poor laborers next to nothing. They lived well on the sufferings of their fellow workers, lying in the lap of luxury while the poor were dying of starvation.

These incredible events are happening even today. The Jat Sikhs and others take advantage of the helplessness of the depressed and poor classes and are very sadistic, reducing their workers to dirt and ashes. I see no virtue or humility in their dealings. They choose where, when, and how they remember and apply the

Guru's teachings. These Jat landlords starve the poor workers and give that money to the gurdwaras to represent themselves as rich and famous in society. Giving to charity is very good but not at the expense of the poor, which is sin and immorality, not moral virtue. They scorn the poor workers and most of them have segregated minds. They call the poor every name under the sun. They are suffering from poverty of conscience. They forget about equality and brotherhood, the teachings of Guru Nanak. They forget that God is watching over them all the time and they cannot deceive God as they do the poor workers. They have a trace of superiority in their attitude, but they are not superior in the eyes of God. They betray the good teaching of the Guru. Each of us should turn the searchlight inward, think carefully, and purify our hearts. I don't relish writing this, and I ask for forgiveness if I'm wrong, but I'm fanatic about truth, and the truth must be told. By following the teachings of Guru Nanak, they can make the world around them beautiful and peaceful.

CHAPTER NINETEEN

THE STRUGGLE FOR A PASSPORT

It was the right time. I was living in Boota Mandi, not far from the civil courts in Jalandhar, and I started inquiring about application forms for my passport. An agent outside the court told me that the application form would cost forty rupees. This was too much. It was blackmail. The next day I tried another agent, but he wanted forty-five rupees. I was furious because these forms were government property and should have cost nothing. I went to the passport window in the civil courts building. A clerk came to the window and I asked him for application forms for the passport, but he told me he didn't have forms. I accused him of selling the forms to the agents rather than giving them to me directly.

The head clerk overheard my conversation and gently told me that I would get into trouble by accusing people like that. I bluntly told him that I didn't have forty-five rupees to buy the forms from an outside agent, but I had enough time to go to Delhi to get them myself. It would cost me only ten rupees for the return train fare. I asked the clerk to at least give me the address of the passport office in Delhi. He calmly told me that I didn't have to travel the two hundred miles to Delhi. If I could manage to get to Hoshiarpur, I could get the forms there. Hoshiarpur was only thirty miles from Jalandhar.

MY TRIP TO HOSHIARPUR

The next day, I took an early train and reached Hoshiarpur around eight o'clock in the morning. I wandered around, taking my time arriving at the civil courts on foot. It was 9:30 when I walked in, but no one was there. The place looked like a ghost town. Soon I saw a dim light in one of those wooden shops in the extreme corner of the courtyard. I went there to ask when the court opened. I saw a young man neatly dressed inside the shop. There was another problem I was very much aware of: shopkeepers in India think its bad luck if the first customer or person they meet in the morning doesn't buy anything, and they curse the customer for it. Knowing I was a bad customer, I asked him hesitantly if he would mind telling me why the court wasn't open. I had come all the way from Nakodar to be a witness in a friend's case.

He said to me, "You know there's a religious fair up in the mountains, and everybody's gone up there. It's a holiday today. You're mistaken about the court."

I quickly responded with, "If it's a holiday, what are you doing here?"

Instead of answering fully, he winked at me, indicating that I should look at the big board hanging a little high in front of the shop. I lifted my eyes and read, "Buy passport application forms and get them typed here." This soothed my mind and body. It was like medicine for my soul. I was happy that I was able to be a customer for him, so I told him jokingly that I had forms, but had left them at home. Otherwise, I would have paid him to type them.

He said quickly that he could give me forms and type them. I agreed, and he typed the forms and put a legal stamp of ten rupees on the form. So, he asked for twenty rupees total, which was a bargain. He told me to take the passport application to the Jalandhar passport office and file it there. One of my friends, Ram Murthi from Abadpur, Jalandhar, came to the window. To my surprise, he was working there. I asked him to take care of the forms and gave him one rupee. He hesitated at first then took the money.

KEEPING MY SECRET
I didn't tell anybody, not even Nasib Kaur, that I had applied for a passport. I was living at Jalandhar, pretending to attend college. In the meantime, I took private tuition with an English professor, Ved Prakashan Munshi of DAV College, for two months, and then for another two months with the chemistry professor Adher Prasad of Doaba College. Those studies did me good at a later stage. I told my father this tuition cost money, and he hesitantly supported me.

After a month or so, a policeman came to my house in Nakodar. Without knowing the reason, my father gave him a rupee and turned him away. The reason the village people didn't like policemen was because a police visit gave one a reputation for having done something wrong. After some months, the policeman came again and my father turned him away again with a rupee, but my father was worried about me. Why were the police looking for me? A neighbor woman named Muni Devi met the policemen and asked him the reason for his repeated visit. Everyone suspected that I must have done something terribly wrong. The policeman told the lady I had applied for a passport and he had to make some inquiries.

Muni Devi told my mother, my wife, and everyone else in the village about the passport. This news sent a shockwave through my family. My father was furious and exasperated that I could take such a big step. They'd never even sent me to the next village; how could I think of going abroad? He sent three of his friends to Jalandhar to look for me and bring me back home. Finally, one of them, who happened to be a guru of my brother Shenker Dutt, found me resting under a mango tree in Nehru Garden. First, he gave me the good news I'd been waiting for, that my wife had given birth to a baby girl. Then he told me that my father wanted to see me immediately. I told him I would go back on Saturday to see my father and baby.

When I got there, my mother was crying. My wife was weeping. My father was angry. He accused me of dodging him and shouted that he'd sent me to Jalandhar to study, not to get a passport. He wanted to know who had advised me to do this. Who had helped me go the wrong way and waste my life and theirs? With a harsh and angry voice, he expressed his disapproval and threatened to tell the police I was a communist. He promised he would do everything he could to stop me from getting the passport.

I talked to my wife and kissed our precious baby softly on her forehead. I listened to her loving, tender voice making our daughter feel warm, safe, and nurtured. We decided to call her by a lovely name,

AN ONWARD JOURNEY

Kamlesh Kumari. I explained my problems and helped Nasib Kaur calm down. By coincidence, I had applied for my passport the same day my daughter was born, September 1, 1953, and I believed this new face would change my luck.

SUCCESS AT LAST

At that time, to get a passport I had to show at least ten thousand rupees in my bank account and some landowners had to vouch for my character, that I was a good person. Our bank manager knew me very well, so I approached him and asked whether he could give me a certificate saying that I had ten thousand rupees in my account. I suggested that he could shift the money from my father's account to my account. He asked if my father knew about this, and I said no. He replied that this would be illegal, and we could both land in jail, plus I would lose my job for good. After hearing this, I begged him not to tell my father about our conversation. My heart broke and I thought for a while that I wouldn't succeed in getting a passport. For the next few weeks, my father and I didn't see eye to eye.

In the meantime, news about my going to UK had spread like wildfire in my village and the surrounding villages. My father's cousin and his friends approached him asking if I could help their uneducated sons apply for passports. My father was in a fix. I stopped eating, filled with resentment about my father's determination not to help me. I talked to a couple of my distant uncles who happened to be his good friends. Blasa Rai and Dave Ram were in Basra and Baghdad in Iraq, and they advised my father that I was doing the right thing. They coaxed him, on top of all the pressure from his friends, customers, and relatives to help their illiterate sons.

AN ONWARD JOURNEY

Finally, one day my father took me to the bank, opened an account under my name, and deposited the required amount of money. Then, a Jat Sikh friend, Maha Singh of Budipind, who lived about a mile from my village, offered to help me and told me I was doing the right thing by going to the UK (because he had been there). He came to my house to set a date to go to the *tehsil* in Nakodar. At the same time, one of our customers, Narsi Ram, was visiting us. He overheard our talk with Maha Singh. Narsi Ram started shouting that his land was useless if we didn't let him help us. He had bought some land recently in Nurmahal. My father laughingly told him, "Okay, go and waste your time running around the offices and the *tehsil*." My problem of getting character references was solved, and finally, after one month, I got my passport from Shimla in early December 1953.

CHAPTER TWENTY

A PARENT'S DILEMMA

My father was extremely worried about who would look after me abroad if I got sick. Who would give me money in a foreign country? He was very concerned about my unknown future. One day he told me all about his worries, that he wasn't happy about my going to the UK. Then he found out an old relative of our neighbor had been living there for the last twenty years and I could go to him. The next day, he came with a proposal. He pointed to my distant cousin and asked me if I knew him. I replied that of course I knew him very well.

"If you know him very well," said my father, "then apply for his passport and take him with you. If both you live together in the UK, then our worries will be less, if not over. You can look after each other in times of sickness or trouble."

This was another big project for me. Shenker Rai was my distant cousin and had only made it to fifth grade in school. His father Rulda Rai was an obedient but illiterate person, my father's cousin. My father always thought it was his responsibility to help all his cousins. He viewed it as charitable work for the people in the village and its surroundings, and they respected him. But he always ordered me to do everything for other people, because at that time I was the only person who was a little bit educated. I could travel on my bike, and since I was trustworthy and willing, I became my father's right-hand man. So, I ran back and forth to Jalandhar, twenty miles away, with Shenker Rai to get his photo taken, complete all the formalities, and finally apply for his passport. Everybody in the village knew I had my passport and I wasn't attending college. I was staying at home most of the time, at Nakodar, and my father used me to do his business work. Once or twice a week, I was told late at night that I must catch a train in the early morning to Ludhiana. Our workers used to take leather bundles to the train station and put them on the train. All I had to do was to bring the money home safely. One day my father told me I had earned my fare to the UK.

Other people, like Lali Ram, asked me to help them apply for a passport. I was busier than ever, running to places to do things for villagers and obey my father's orders. Several villagers found me busy, so they got help from other people and paid them or hired agents. Between 1954 and 1955, several illiterate people went to the UK. I was getting impatient waiting for Shenker Rai's passport. Finally, after few weeks, it arrived. The next step was booking passage to England. My father wrote a letter to Shiv Raj in Delhi asking him to help me book seats. Airfare cost about one hundred pounds but traveling by ship was cheaper. So, I bought two tickets for sixty pounds each to Southampton. We would be sailing from Bombay on the *Battery*, a big Polish ship.

AN ONWARD JOURNEY

A PASSPORT FOR NASIB KAUR

After booking my trip, I was invited by Shiv Raj's friends, Priti Singh and Bhag Singh, to Karol Bagh for dinner. They started talking about my wife, her health, and her future. I had no proper answer for them, and I bluntly said I would think about it. I was not working at the time, nor sure of my future in England, and my father was not willing to send my wife and child along.

My brother-in-law Shiv Raj, who was seated next to me, said rather sternly, "Why not think now, before you go home?" He stressed that no one in my family would help her at all. He also pointed out that getting a passport hardly takes one month, and it took me a year because my family didn't want to help me. What he said sounded harsh to me, but it was all true and I've been grateful to him all my life for stating the facts. They always worried about my wife, that I was leaving her behind in a state of illness.

I didn't answer Shiv Raj right then, but all the way back to Nakodar on the bus, I thought about nothing but my wife and child. It was torture. I felt depressed. I reached home in the late evening, and that night I didn't sleep well. Early in the morning, about five o'clock, Nasib Kaur got up to milk the cows and sweep the house. I asked her to tell my mother she was sick. But she refused, knowing that she would be in a lot of trouble for lying and lose my parents' trust. Later in the morning, I asked my mother politely to look after my child as I wanted to take my wife to Jalandhar to see the doctor for a checkup. She didn't agree to help and said that our regular hakim, Mohat Ram, was coming to examine my father and could check Nasib Kaur, too. I bluntly told my mother that if she couldn't look after my child, I would go to the neighbors. Then she rushed to me and grabbed the child from me. "Come back soon. I can't keep the child all day," said my mother in a loud voice.

I winked at Nasib Kaur, who had heard the argument, signaling her to dress and get ready. We took the bus after walking nearly two miles to the bus station. I knew the photo studio in Jalandhar, my favorite one on Grand Trunk Road, not far from the bus station. I asked the photographer for passport-sized photos and paid him, and we hurried back to Nakodar Road to catch the bus home. We were worried that mother wouldn't be happy with us if we were late.

After reaching Nakodar, we hired a rickshaw to take us close to home quickly. On the road, we saw my father sitting in a tonga, on the way home from town. He saw us sitting in the rickshaw. We suspected this wouldn't be good for us. After reaching home, he told my mother that we were enjoying life and fooling around in a rickshaw. I suspect my father was jealous as he hadn't ridden in a rickshaw when he was young and always walked on foot for long distances. I heard them talking while I was sitting on the roof. Mother didn't waste any time confronting me, and she immediately shouted that we were using her so we could go out merrymaking. I laughed and told my mother that my father would have been very happy to see my wife sitting in a rickshaw with some high-caste idiot. He couldn't tolerate both of us sitting in the rickshaw. He was angry with mother for telling me everything he'd said to her and insisted he didn't mean anything by it. That was life in those days with old-fashioned people, who grew up under suppression and misery before the twentieth century. They weren't allowed to think due to constant oppression by evils.

Before leaving home for the UK, I applied for a passport for my wife and baby and asked a trustworthy friend to make sure she got it without my parents' knowledge.

PART II

CHAPTER TWENTY ONE

PREPARATION FOR THE UNITED KINGDOM
1954

Leaving my near and dear ones and the village where I grew up was very difficult. It was a challenging situation for me. It was an extraordinary journey from a remote village in northern India to the United Kingdom, a journey no one in my village had attempted before 1954. Going abroad was uncommon for a young man at that time.

My mother was still unwilling to let me go, and she didn't like the idea of me going to the UK. She offered to give me all the money my father had put into her bank account if I changed my mind and stayed home. She often said to me that only poor people went away for work. Why should I leave home? She believed I didn't need to work since my father was well off. My father was very perplexed about my desire to go to an unknown place in a faraway land, and worried about my poor health. Shenker Dutt wanted me to go to Delhi and pursue work as a junior clerk in a government office as many of my community members did. I wasn't brought up living in a tiny bedroom and working in a crowded city like Delhi. I had seen government servants sleeping on the floor and two to three children sharing one bed. This was beyond me. I'd compared my life to that of these Delhi babus (clerks) and decided that I had a much easier and better life.

CONFUSION AND EMOTION

My mind was made up. My passport was ready. I had booked my passage and finally got permission from my father to go to the UK. The day of departure was drawing closer, and I found myself feeling confused. Everything seemed so difficult. I wasn't leaving my house or my village on my own sweet will. I was driven out by my circumstances, by a need to get away from Brahmanism and other evils; by my own consciousness, grit, and masculine ego; and by a need to stand on my own two feet, earn a living, and support my family.

I was feeling very sad because I feared in my heart that I would never see my village or home again. I looked at the fruit trees I'd planted and pondered who would be eating the bananas and oranges when they ripened. I went up on the roof and looked out at the horizon and the beautiful landscape. I loved nature. I loved the rich soil, the greenness of the crops, the yellow flowers of the mustard plants in the fields. The landscape had changed to a lush green that smelled so fresh. I glanced at the faraway, small, dense clump of trees where I'd spent all my lonely hours when I was young.

My father made sure I had enough of everything. He gave me over two thousand rupees in cash and a wardrobe of six shirts, four pairs of pants, a suit, and an overcoat, all custom-made by a local tailor. I did like some of the clothes, but others I didn't.

Finally, I left home on March 1, 1954, in the early

morning to catch the 7:00 a.m. train to Ludhiana. All my friends and neighbors came to the railroad platform to see me off and say goodbye. My distant cousin Shenker Rai joined me as planned. When the time came to depart and the engineer blew the final whistle, it was heartbreaking to leave the place. I was so grief-stricken that I almost cried. I kept looking back again and again. Deep in my heart, I was distressed and skeptical of going abroad, leaving my wife, my baby of only a few months, and my parents behind. The train moved on, and we switched trains for Delhi at Ludhiana.

In Delhi, we stayed with Shiv Raj for two nights and bought train tickets to Bombay. Shiv Raj and Ram Dyal, came to see us off at the Delhi railroad platform and stowed our luggage safely on the train. Shiv Raj was very emotional, and his eyes were full of tears when he shook hands with me, said goodbye, and wished us good luck on our long journey. My own condition was not good, and a feeling of depression overtook me as I moved closer every minute to the unknown land, leaving my home, friends, and relatives behind.

FORCED TO BRIBE

This was our first trip to Bombay, and we had no experience. We were on our own now. The journey was very tiresome and boring as we met people who spoke different languages and dressed differently. We felt like foreigners in our own country.

The next day, I thought we were in or near Gujarat state. A ticket inspector boarded the train after midnight and demanded our tickets. After examining them, he shouted, "Whose luggage is this? These trunks are too big and too heavy." His behavior was very rude. He was speaking in a different mixed language and ordered us to get off the train at the next station. We got scared and ended up paying one hundred rupees each.

Finally, we reached the Bombay train station in the early morning. Shiv Raj had given us the address of a Punjabi hotel to stay at. We hired a horse cart and reached the hotel. Here we met two other boys from my area in Punjab. They were also going to the United Kingdom, and we learned from them that our ship was late by four days for some reason. During these four days, my cousin Shenker Rai became acquainted with the employees and agents of the hotel. I asked him repeatedly not to indulge in any private talk with strangers, but he didn't heed my advice.

On the day we were to sail, we took a taxi to the Bombay dock along with our Punjabi friends. Upon arriving at the dock, we had to pass inspection with immigration or other authorities. I was in front, and the first of the four of us. I boarded the big ship and waited for the others at the top of the gangway. My Punjabi friends told me that Shenker Rai hadn't been cleared because of his bogus passport. I was at my wits' end. I struggled to understand as I had personally applied for his passport and everything had been done legally. I hurried back to the immigration authorities. When I asked for an explanation, they demanded to see my passport and bluntly told me that it was also fake. Without listening to me, they put both of us in the van and took us to the city police station. We were made to sit on the bench in the veranda in front of the station. Now my distant cousin was panicking and didn't know what to do.

After two hours of waiting, one of Shenker Rai's

friends from the hotel appeared and asked us what we were doing there. After hearing our ordeal, he told us the matter would be solved if we gave money to the immigration authorities. We paid four hundred rupees each and our passports were cleared and given back to us to board the ship. This was the result of friendship with strangers and crooks. Before even boarding the ship, we'd lost five hundred rupees each. I was worried that Shenker Rai was nothing but trouble and that my father had made a grave mistake by pressing me to take him along. I didn't know how it would go and the situation incensed me greatly.

A MISERABLE MAIDEN JOURNEY

Finally, the ship sailed from Bombay on March 10, and we felt a deep solace in our hearts. It wasn't a pleasant journey at all as we'd had only trouble since we left Delhi. Perhaps it was because we were plain, ignorant village boys who knew little about the outside world. Shenker Rai's arrogant and stubborn attitude and behavior was overwhelming. There was no illusion in my mind that his attire and his interaction with strangers had led to our humiliation and the loss of our money. He had good shoes and clothes in his suitcase, but he was wearing *chappels* (sandals) and a shirt with rolled-up sleeves like a villager. This indicated that he was a simple, uneducated, and backward village boy and his so-called friends took advantage of his situation. I was furious that I was losing money because of his stupidity and stubbornness.

However, the ship sailed on. There were rough seas and sometimes massive ocean waves splashed onto the deck. I didn't get seasick, but I had a lot of headaches because of the strong smell of diesel. People who were used to traveling, especially the Europeans, enjoyed it. They were dancing in dance halls and swimming in the pool. I was tongue-tied because I was shy. I wasn't used to the Western food, so I had to eat fruit and cookies for most of the journey. I wasn't used to handling forks and knives, because in Indian villages we just used our fingers as utensils. This also added to my misery of sitting at a dining table among strange people. The atmosphere was charged with embarrassment and I felt uncomfortable the entire time. I tried to eat in my cabin or sit on the deck to pass the time. I couldn't reply if someone tried to speak to me because I felt shy and nothing could bring me to conquer my shyness.

The first stop after three or four days of sailing on the Arabian Sea was Aden (Yemen), and we were warned about pickpockets and advised to leave expensive items in our lockers. It was a tax-free port and things were cheap. I'd never owned a wristwatch in my life and was badly in need of one. So, I opted to buy it. The shopkeeper gave me a bargain on a box camera, and I fell for it, knowing very well that I shouldn't spend money, but I saw the necessity of these things, especially the wristwatch. My distant cousin bought nothing but a bottle of whiskey. When we returned to our cabin on the ship, the first thing he did was open his whiskey. He didn't like it and emptied the whole bottle in the sink.

We proceeded through the Red Sea to the Suez Canal. On the right was Saudi Arabia, a big desert full of big heaps of sand. At that time, I didn't know that under the sand was a lot of black gold (oil). And on the left was Egypt with a little bit of greenery here and there. Then we stopped at the Port Side. I did go out for two hours, but I didn't buy anything except a postcard and wrote to my parents, a popular saying: *"Jo Sukh apnee Chuvarrae na Bulkh na Bukharae,"* meaning "East or West, home is the best." But Shenker Rai bought another bottle of whiskey, and once again, he dumped it in the sink. Then we entered the Mediterranean Sea and stopped at the island of Malta. We also stopped at Gibraltar, near Spain, before reaching our destination seaport, Southampton, England, and we thanked God. It was our maiden journey over the sea, and for us Indian village boys who had never crossed the sea before, it was horrible and unrelenting. It took us twenty-one days from Bombay to Southampton, and I lost twelve pounds, weighing only a meager ninety-one pounds at the end. But, most importantly, our arrival in England was a day of deliverance. It was a day of full freedom from Brahmanism and casteism. It was a day of rejoicing and it was day of thanking God Almighty. We were free at last, but at the same time, I missed my parents, wife, and baby. In the evening we boarded a train to Glasgow and traveled all night, five hundred miles. We reached Glasgow, Scotland, in the early morning hours.

On my way to the UK via ship (1954)

CHAPTER
TWENTY TWO

MY JOURNEY TO THE UNKNOWN
MARCH 1954

Finally, Shenker Rai and I reached our destination, Glasgow Central Station, in the early morning. The platform was long and quiet, and I thought the train slowed down with a purpose, but soon I looked outside and noticed a big sign for Glasgow Central Station. The platform's atmosphere was totally different from the hustle and bustle of the Indian platform, and there were no porters in red shirts. I was still dreaming of the sight of red shirts and vendors selling tea and cookies on the platform. There was no jostling or pushing to get on or off the train; everything was so peaceful, and I took my time to disembark. The station was picturesque, with a high ceiling and plenty of accommodations for passengers to move around. There were benches everywhere and a big clock hung on the wall near the train schedules. A beautiful egg-shaped ticket office with lots of windows was situated near the entrance. Soon I noticed a taxi and hurried to catch it like in India. But the driver pointed to a sign, so we got in line to wait.

When our turn came, the driver helped us load our luggage into the taxi, then pulled away. I was excited to see the beautiful buildings around the station. To my surprise, the driver didn't ask me the address of my destination, and after about ten minutes, he stopped the taxi in the street and asked me for the number of the street we wanted to go to. I didn't understand him, and I handed over the airmail letter with an address on it that I was carrying with me. He drove a few blocks further, charged the fare and let us out at 216 Nicholson Street, Gorbals, Glasgow. He had a profound knowledge of Indian and Pakistani people and knew that most of them lived on Nicholson Street, an older area of Glasgow. We were surprised that he knew where we were going.

The building was an old three or four-story gray stone building with four apartments on each side. So, we took our luggage and went up to the second floor, checking the name on each of the apartments. Our distant uncle Chand Lal was waiting in the doorway for us in his sleeping clothes. He must have seen us from the window after hearing the taxi arrive. So finally, we reached our destination a month after leaving home. It was clear to us that it was better to come by air than by sea. It wasn't worthwhile to save forty pounds for ship fare as the journey was too long and tiresome and there were a lot of hungry vultures in Bombay, like the immigration officers and other crooks, ready to eat the flesh of ignorant and new people.

At breakfast, we talked about the welfare of the people in India and hurried to sleep on the beds that Chand Lal had placed in the big living room. The next day, visitors started coming to meet us newcomers and learn about Punjab. In 1954, only a dozen people from my community were living in Glasgow, and all of them were older than we were. They had left their families in

Punjab fifteen to twenty years before and never gone back. It was comforting to us to meet people from our own community in a foreign land.

After a week of resting, we started talking about work available in Glasgow, and Chand Lal told us that there were no factories there. All his friends sold clothes door-to-door and we should do the same. We weren't fit for the job since we didn't speak fluent English and had little money. He took us to a shop and bought two lightweight suitcases for twenty pounds each. He then took us to a Pakistani clothing warehouse and bought a few shirts, ties, socks and ladies' clothes, and we each ended up forty pounds in debt.

Luckily enough, things weren't expensive in those days and one penny had a lot of buying power. A loaf of bread used to cost one to two pence and traveling in Glasgow from one terminal to another cost only two pence. Vegetables were quite cheap as well. We were new and didn't know much about fancy foods, so we ate lots of cookies, tea, and Indian dal and roti (curry and chapati).

A LICENSE TO SELL CLOTHING

We had to learn the English names of clothing, which were all new to us: blouses, skirts, nylons, etc. Then Chand Lal took us to the local police station to apply for a license to sell clothing door-to-door, called a peddler's license. Now we were ready to go out with our suitcases to knock on doors and ask people to buy clothing from us. But it sounded funny to me, as I was too shy and in a foreign country with a foreign language. Should I knock on the back or the front door? Where should I go, what should I say, and how should I behave? I was so shocked; it made no sense to me. I feared I had made a mistake coming to Glasgow. But I didn't know anyone else in the UK and had no choice but to follow the wishes of Chand Lal.

The first day, Shenker Rai and I both went to a village called Uddingston, about ten miles outside Glasgow. We didn't want to do anything, so we rested in a small park. We saw an Indian going around the houses to sell his goods. I followed him from a distance to see what he was doing, going to the front or back door, etc. He knocked on two or three back kitchen doors but had no luck. The Scottish ladies simply opened the door, said no, then shut the door in his face. This gave me discomfort, but also some encouragement to try my luck. We spent the rest of the day in the park, then went home and told Uncle that we'd tried but couldn't sell anything.

The second day, we did the same: played cards, then went home and told our uncle that we'd had no luck. I was keeping account of every penny I was spending on fare, etc., and we were losing money every day. It was a challenging situation. The third day, we went to a newly built town called Birkenshaw, and both of us took an oath to go around the houses and knock on doors no matter what. My cousin went south, and I went north in the village. Scared and anxious, I knocked on the back_ kitchen door. Nothing happened. Then, after one minute, I knocked again and a gracious older lady with an apron on opened the door. She asked me if I had men's socks and invited me in. She told me I looked tired and gave me a cup of tea and a cookie. I was happy that the lady was so nice and let me into her house. After finishing the tea, I showed her the goods I was carrying. She bought a shirt, an apron, and two pairs of socks and gave me the money I asked for. I left the house and started looking for my cousin to give him the good news. We sat down in the park and started checking the prices of the goods I sold. To my surprise, I'd sold them at a loss. I'd forgotten the real prices.

A letter came from my mother begging me to come back. It was written by my brother, who'd never written a letter in his life. Despite the many mistakes, I made sense of it. My mother said that I'd had enough vacation and had seen the world, and now she wanted me to come back because she missed me too much. I wasn't happy in Glasgow, but I was more and more tied up with everyday life and had less and less money, and I remembered my agonizing days in India.

We used to get one or two visitors every day. We kept pleading with the visitors for some real labor, and we had no interest in selling things. Shenker Rai never made any sales and had no knowledge of English, either. About six weeks had passed and we were worried. These were dreadful and gloomy days. We were desperate for work. We were like lost ships at sea.

SHENKER RAI FINDS A JOB
A friend, Mangu Ram of Sanma, came early in the morning, woke us up and asked us to go with him in his van to a town called Inverness for a chance to get employment there. I didn't go because I was too weak, but Shenker Rai went and was hired as a laborer building dams near Inverness. I kept trying to sell clothes, but with little success.

One day I was waiting for a bus on a famous Glasgow strip, Duke Street, and I smelled something. The smell was familiar to me and I became inquisitive to find out where it was coming from. I deliberately missed the bus and crossed the road in search of its origin. After spending fifteen minutes walking up and down the street, I saw somebody come out of a big door, the source of the smell. I went inside and a foreman asked me the purpose of my visit. He said that if I was looking for a job, I should come back the next day. After hearing that, I became very hopeful and enthusiastic about getting a job.

I FIND EMPLOYMENT

The next morning, I went back to the place, which was called Miller Tanning Company, and the foreman put me to work with another Scottish worker. It was a job I could handle easily. I wasn't new to leather manufacturing as my father ran a leather company in India and I was quite used to the work and the smell. In 1954, I worked forty-four hours a week and was paid only six and half pounds after tax, cash in an envelope. I opened a bank account and started depositing all my wages. I made it my habit to give the envelope to the bank teller without opening and tell her to deposit it in my account. For my rent and living expenses, I did odd jobs for a few hours when possible and collected my debts. After four or five months, I had a hundred pounds in my account, and I was rich, jumping up and down with joy that I had my own money earned with my own sweat and blood. That was real money and I often multiplied my Scottish pounds by thirteen to convert them to Indian rupees.

TROUBLE WITH MY FATHER

The second letter came from my father. It said that my wife had received her passport. I was happy, but my father wasn't. He accused me of giving him a bad name.

AN ONWARD JOURNEY

He said the villagers and his friends were saying that he'd put his son out and now he was putting his daughter-in-law out, too. I wrote to my father asking him to send my wife and baby to the UK, but he responded asking me to come back. They didn't want to send my wife to Scotland. In the next four months, he wrote some very angry letters. In one, he said that they had four different addresses for me and didn't know which one to write to. In another, he said that my wife couldn't carry my luggage on her head like a porter and move from place to place like I did. They made all kinds of excuses: Fare for the baby cost too much. They could buy a good milk cow with that kind of money. Then my wife wrote that they wanted her to leave the baby with them.

I was fed up with all this idle talk and didn't know what to do. In the meantime, I saved more money and started looking for a house as I didn't like renting. On evenings and weekends, I started looking for a house for sale. All the agents told me the houses were sold although the "for sale" signs were still there. I wasted a lot of time and failed to learn the price of any place. One Sunday morning I was waiting for a bus and a Scottish white person came to the bus stop with an umbrella. I casually asked him whether the house facing us was for sale and questioned why the sale sign was there even though the agent said the house was sold when I asked him. He asked me why I wanted a house if I could rent a single inexpensive room rather than buy a house. In reply, I told him that I was married, and my wife was coming to Glasgow to live with me. He advised me to see a lawyer; otherwise, it would be very hard for me to buy a house as I was a foreigner. I didn't know any lawyers, and he told me to go to Glasgow Square as there were a lot of lawyers there.

The next day I went, and there were a lot of lawyers with funny names I couldn't even pronounce properly. Finally, I settled on one with a simple name, Mr. Risk, and went to the second floor to see him. His secretary, an old lady, came to the window and inquired about my visit. I said I wanted to see Mr. Risk, who was about to go out with his coat on. He walked in and introduced himself. I explained to him that I wanted to buy a house (Condominium). He told me to write down the addresses of the houses I liked and drop a note in his mailbox. He would find the price for me.

I started looking and left two or three addresses in his mailbox. He wrote to me to see him personally for the list of prices. I took a few hours off work to meet with him. He asked me where I worked and why I wanted to buy a house ten miles away when there were a lot of houses available near my job. I told him I liked beautiful Redstone buildings and wanted to live far from Pakistanis and Indians. He told me to forget about Redstone and find a house near my job, which was far from the Gorbals (a densely populated area popular with immigrants) and would save time and money as I was a first-time buyer. His advice opened my eyes. The next day, I found two or three houses for sale in a good area within walking distance of my work. The one I liked had two large bedrooms, one large living room, bathroom, and good-sized kitchen. The bathroom had a nice large water heater and that was very attractive to me since in England, toilets were outside. I asked the lawyer to find the price as I really wanted the house. He wrote back that the price of the house was £350. At the same time, he told me he felt I wouldn't get it as there were too many other buyers. I was disappointed, and I took a half day off from work and went to see the lawyer. I asked him whether the house had sold, and he said it hadn't yet. Then I asked him to pick up the phone and call the agent. I offered to pay £50 down and £5 every month. The agent declined. My second offer was £300, all cash. The agent again declined. I kept making counteroffers, and now my lawyer was sure I was committed to buying the house. After two hours of counteroffers, I managed to settle the price of £350: £250 down and the rest within a year without interest. The initial paperwork was completed and signed.

A few days later, the lawyer told me to meet the agent. I went, and he tried to buy the house from me, giving me £20 profit. I declined and became a little angry. Then he asked me if I liked cats and dogs. I walked away without answering any questions. In a hurry, I told him that I didn't like cats and dogs, and I didn't like bad people either. I went to the lawyer and he gave me the keys to my house.

OUR NEW HOUSE (CONDOMINIUM)

Now I had bought the house with all the savings I had. For furniture, I had to wait for my next payday. I felt bad that I had no money left in the bank. The next day, a friend, Balu Ram of Lallian Klan, met with me and bluffed that he had a good job and the pay was very good. He suggested that I get a job in the factory as there was a lot of work and they needed more men. I quit my job, and the following morning, I expected him to take me to the factory, but he didn't show up. I was still living on Nicholson Street and he was living just across the street. So, I sat near the window, ready to go to work, watching for him to come out. It was a little late, but he did come out and went straight to the bus. I assumed he'd forgotten his promise to take me with him. I ran out of the house and tried to meet him, but

AN ONWARD JOURNEY

I was too late. He caught the bus, and I was left behind. Luckily, another bus of the same number and going to the same destination was approaching. I managed to catch it and went up to the upper deck and sat in the front seat, hoping to see where he got off the bus. The bus crossed the busy streets of the city and turned north of Glasgow. Finally, I saw him get off at the industrial area. I hurried down but got off at the next stop.

I entered the place, a chemical factory. I went to the office and gave my name and address and other information. They gave me a pick and shovel and pointed to me a railroad wagon with instructions to help the Punjabi workers unload the wagons. The open wagon was full of powder salt and had solidified like a stone. The three of us tried hard and managed to empty the wagon by the end of the shift. This was tough and dangerous work compared to the tanning factory. When I went home, my hands were covered in blisters and I was tired. I was feeling sorry that I'd given up my other job for this new one. I was disappointed. I changed my mind and decided to stay home the next day, but I was desperate for money.

I went to work, and the foreman showed me the forty-pound drums and told me to stack them in the other room. Two other Punjabi workers were grinding the chemical and filling the drums with powder. After a couple of hours, my face felt irritated and scratchy. The men shouted at me to wear a mask so I wouldn't get sick. Later, I learned that a man who already worked there was in the hospital. I stopped work for lunch and took the mask off; it was blue. I became very afraid that I would end up in the hospital as well. I was so disappointed and fed up that I went to the office and told them I wanted to quit. I didn't even care if they paid me or not. They insisted I stay as there was a lot of overtime and a lot of money I could make. However, I didn't want to listen. I just wanted to get out of the place. Finally, they gave me twelve hours' wages and I left and took the double-decker bus home.

As usual, I liked to travel on the upper deck, where it was quiet, and no one bothered me. As I was sitting there, my eyes landed on an advertisement in the bus for a bus conductor job with the Glasgow Corporation. I wrote down the address and went home. I washed, changed clothes, and hurried to the Glasgow Corporation office on Bath Street to apply for the job. The same afternoon, I was given a simple arithmetic test and got everything correct. But sadly, the clerk told me that the job had been filled a few hours earlier. I was disheartened and the clerk promised me that the next job available would be mine. I was disappointed and hungry.

THE GLASGOW CORPORATION JOB

I went downstairs, where there was a famous coffee shop, without thinking of the cost. I had two cups of coffee and a piece of cake to fill my belly. I rested there for a while. At the same time, an idea came to my mind: the Glasgow Corporation was big and was responsible for running the city, so they must have had some other jobs available. With this hope, I went back to the window. The clerk asked me if I could work with a pick and shovel. I answered affirmatively, and he gave me the address of a place called Ballston, just outside Glasgow, and told me to report there at 10:00 p.m. Also, he gave me some tokens to travel there. Upon arriving, I saw a swarm of Punjabis, a few of whom I knew. I worked there for three nights. Then, on the fourth day, the foreman held me back and sent everybody home. He gave me a letter from the Glasgow Corporation and told me to go there that afternoon. The letter said to collect the uniform and start training the next day. This job was for an underground train conductor instead of a bus conductor, which didn't involve issuing tickets. I was happy that I'd found work quickly as I was desperate for money.

After receiving the keys from my lawyer, I wrote to my father that I'd bought a house. Now his daughter-in-law had a permanent place to live and wouldn't have to follow me here and there. It was the beginning of July 1955. The next day I moved to 91 Roslea Drive, Dennistoun. I received three quilts and sheets from my friends. I cleaned one bedroom thoroughly and bought a bag of coal to heat the room. I was tired and went to bed early. At about 11:30 p.m., I heard a noise at my door and woke up. I was dead scared that somebody was trying to break my main door. I didn't know what to do. I didn't have a stick or a knife in the house. Finally, I saw a small coal shovel and I picked it up and went to the door. There was a little peephole in the door, and I looked through it and saw a red-haired woman.

A PIOUS AND GRACIOUS LADY

I was relieved and opened the door cautiously, still holding the small shovel in my hand. The lady said she was sorry for waking me up. "I'm nearly done, and you can go to bed," she said. I asked her what she was doing, and it turned out she was polishing my door and cleaning the brass doorknob with Brasso (a cleaning product).

The next day when I came home from work, she

was sweeping the stairs. I had a talk with her. I had bought the house and I was the owner, so it was my job to clean the stairs. She said I didn't have to worry about the stairs as she had been doing it herself for a year, ever since the last owner moved out. I was impressed that she was so gracious and saw God in her. I took some change and notes from my trouser pocket and asked her to take some money. She refused, but after I insisted, she took half a crown. That's one-eighth of a pound, a very small amount. This really touched my heart. I went in the house and burst into tears just thinking that she wasn't from my family or my country, not related to me in any way. Who was she? God had showed her mercy in many ways. She was my neighbor, Mrs. Burnett. Soon I began to meet other tenants coming and going from their houses and became acquainted.

July was the month of a two-week holiday in the UK. Three fellows from Birmingham, England, heard that I had bought a house. They were from my village. Without informing me, they came to Glasgow by bus. I was at work. When I came home, they were sitting at the corner of the street, waiting for me. They were new to the country and stayed with me for a week. They made enough noise day and night to upset the neighbors. The neighbors weren't sure what was going to happen, and they were worried. My next-door neighbor started advertising in the paper to sell her house and she kept the ad going for a few months. One Indian friend from Delhi met me in Glasgow Square when he was switching buses to go home. I asked him what he was doing there, and he told me he'd gone to see a house in Dennistoun, and I told him that I lived in there and gave him my address to visit sometime. He was looking at the house next door to mine. I was upset that my neighbor had put her house on the market because of me. By chance I ran into Mrs. Burnett, explained my visitors, and told her that my wife and baby were coming from India to join me. After a few days, she took her house off the market and I felt very happy.

My Wife's Passport Photograph (1954)

CHAPTER TWENTY THREE

THE BEST GIFT FROM MY FATHER
SEPTEMBER 1955

My Father was adamant not to send my wife and baby to a faraway, unknown place. He didn't know anything about Scotland as he'd never gone to school. He didn't trust me and wanted me to come home. In fact, he missed me too much. When he learned that I'd bought a house, he sent my wife and baby to Delhi, to her cousin's brother, Shiv Raj, so they could stay with the family for a few days before flying to the UK. My brother-in-law booked her seat to London and sent me a telegram about her arrival at the London airport.

Shiv Raj was worried about Nasib Kaur because she was a remote village girl who had never traveled much in Punjab and had no education, and now she was traveling alone to a foreign country with a baby. He did all he could, said a prayer for her safe travels, and wrote a letter to the airport authorities giving my full address in Scotland in case I was late to receive her. He made sure she had enough money in case of an emergency. He took her to the airport and gave a note to the stewardess to give her special care as she couldn't speak English. He booked her seat with British Airways because he thought that company was trustworthy and took better care of its passengers.

The plane stopped at Karachi Airport in Pakistan and picked up a few passengers. She was sitting behind the Pakistani passengers, and during the journey they found her very quiet and scared. To cheer her up, they started talking to the baby. Then they asked her where she was from. She said Nakodar in Punjab. The Pakistani travelers were from a village called Mahuwal and asked her if she knew or had ever heard of it. She told them she'd lived in Nai-Abadi, less than a mile from Mahuwal, near the railroad track and told them my father's name. They were happy to know about my father and his welfare and told Nasib Kaur that my father used to buy a lot of wheat from them every year when they were in India before the partition. They took care of her when she needed anything for herself or the baby. Knowing they were there she became a little more relaxed and time passed without any problem.

I received a telegram well in advance from Shiv Raj and planned to take the early morning train from Glasgow to London, a four-hundred-mile journey, on the day of her arrival in the late evening. Then I thought it might be better to travel by night train in case the morning train was late. After reaching London, I had to inquire in the railroad office about the airport because this was my first visit to London. At that time, I didn't know anyone in London, so I traveled there by double-decker bus. In the afternoon, well before the plane's arrival, I reached the London airport. There was no Heathrow airport then; it was only a set of blueprints. The airport was not very big then. I traveled a lot on buses in the airport's surrounding area to find an Indian restaurant or at least an Indian who could tell me more about the place and the airport. In those days there were hardly any Indians or Pakistanis living in that area. However, when the plane arrived, I walked close to where the people were coming out after immigration and customs. I think I was the only Indian waiting there.

The Pakistanis from Mahuwal were the first to come out and when they saw me, they could tell that I was waiting for my wife and baby. They asked my name and told me that she would come out soon and that she and the baby were quite fine. They relieved some tension and I felt a little relaxed. After ten or fifteen minutes, Nasib Kaur came out with a small suitcase and the baby. She was feeling shy as usual. I tried to take the baby from her, but she gave me the suitcase instead because the baby was sleeping. I didn't say much and hurried to catch a taxi as I didn't want to miss the train to Glasgow. Luckily enough, we reached Euston Railway Station only half an hour early. It was a misty and rainy day and we got an empty compartment on the train. We traveled all night and the train took eleven or twelve hours to reach Glasgow. In the morning, we took a taxi home.

It was the morning of September 8, 1955. My wife Nasib Kaur and my daughter Kamlesh had arrived in Glasgow, Scotland, from India. Baby Kamlesh was now two years old and my wife was nearly twenty-three. We'd been separated for about seventeen months, a long time. I thanked God and my father, for it was the best gift I'd ever received from my father. It freed my wife and me to live our own life and mind our own business. This was the start of a fresh life for the two of us and for our little child. We were truly in a free country where people were civilized. We were happy to be far away from evil Hindu Brahmanism and the

Muslim and Sikh communities that had treated us badly and hated us. We had full freedom to do as we pleased. We were independent, empowered to choose where and how we would live in all seasons of life. We were both very happy and it was a gorgeous day.

CHAPTER
TWENTY FOUR

OUR NEW LIFE IN SCOTLAND
SEPTEMBER 1955

Living in the district of Dennistoun, Glasgow, we began our new lives. It was the start of a new chapter in a truly free country.

On arriving home, I took my wife into the bedroom, the only room that had furniture in it. She immediately asked if I had any milk in the house. There was a bottle of milk sitting near the window, where it was a little cold. I didn't have a refrigerator yet. She wanted to heat the milk for Kamlesh. I took her into the kitchen, where I had an old portable gas burner, and I heated the milk for the child. She asked me who lived in the other rooms. I realized she didn't know I'd bought the house. Perhaps my father hadn't been in any hurry to tell her. I had written previously that I lived in a rented room. She must have had the impression that I was still renting.

EXCITEMENT
After she finished feeding the baby, I walked her through the living room, bedroom, and bathroom. I told her that all the rooms belonged to her and she could do whatever she wanted with them. She didn't

say anything, but her face turned red. After a while she speculated that the rent must be high, which confirmed that she didn't know I had bought the house. I told her I'd bought it only a few weeks before and all the rooms were hers. Her face flushed and beamed with joy. Seeing her excited and happy, I felt full of energy, vitality, and a sense of inner peace. The frustration that had oppressed me for so long was gone. I felt a wave of relief wash over me. God had come to my aid and laid the foundation of our lives in Scotland. He had sown the seeds of self-respect, integrity, independence, and justice that had never been possible in India, where we were surrounded by Brahmanism and other hatred.

I had to go to work. I was on second shift, working as a conductor on an underground rail in Glasgow. We had a penny gas meter, so I showed my wife how to operate it and how to light the gas burner. We didn't have a phone then and we were using coal to heat the house. Washing machines hadn't yet been invented. I changed my clothes and put on my uniform. She was impressed by the uniform and asked me where I was going in these new clothes. I told her I was going to work and would be back late in the evening. So, this is how we started our new life in Scotland.

The next day, she opened her suitcase and gave me twenty film song records. I also saw an Indian shawl that wasn't folded properly but instead had a big knot at one end. She told me that my mother had made the knot, so she wouldn't forget the message she wanted to tell me. The message was that my long absence from home was having a profound effect on my father. He went to the post office a mile and a half away to check the mail. If he didn't hear from me, he came back feeling tired and sad, sat quietly outside the house, and didn't talk to anybody for hours. My mother asked me to write a letter to my father every week.

On the weekends I brought my wages home instead of depositing them in the bank and gave them to my wife. She refused to take them, but then I explained to her jokingly that I was there to work, and her job was to spend. She was adamant about not taking any money or responsibility, but I wanted to give her a responsibility. I didn't insist but left the money in the bedroom so at least she could see the pound notes and change and get acquainted with the Scottish money. I knew she was a small Indian village girl who'd never been to school, and now she was in an advanced foreign country, far from her mother and near and dear ones. Under all these circumstances, I wanted her to be happy so she wouldn't get homesick or complain to my parents.

A NEW EYE DOCTOR
I knew she had bad eyes, so after a few weeks, when she was completely rested from her long journey and its jet lag, I took her to the Glasgow Royal Infirmary a mile from our house. The doctor examined her eyes, performed x-rays, and so on. He gave her drops to put in her eyes every night and asked her to report back in two weeks. They gave her a pair of eyeglasses and asked her to look at certain objects through them. Hesitantly, I told her not to worry if she couldn't see through the glasses, but she said she could see much better. I became emotional at hearing such words. My eyes were full of tears. I did my best to hold back, but a few drops fell down my cheeks. She was happy and her face turned red, but I was even happier. I felt that I had gotten everything I wanted by coming to Scotland. My joy knew no bounds and I wrote letter to our families

right away to give them the good news. I was thanking God day and night that he had come to our aid. Her eyesight wasn't perfect, but it was a lot better than it had been in India when she was almost blind. She was in a much better position to handle things, which gave me motivation and happiness.

SHOPPING

We used to go to the south side of the city to Indian shop, four miles away, around the Gorbals every weekend. One day, I asked her to look at the bus number. She had no clue what I was saying. She didn't bother to look for any number on the buses. Instead, she was in the habit of walking behind or beside me, knowing nothing about where I was going. I wanted to break that habit so she could become independent and behave responsibly. This was a big task, breaking her years-old habit of dependence on me, so every time we went out, I asked her to look for the bus number.

One day, she said, "All I can see is a big line." She didn't know that was the number one. When we got home, I gave her a pen and paper to draw that number. She thought I was joking and walked away, leaving the pen and paper on the table. I didn't want to press her or argue with her as she was alone and becoming homesick, but she had enough to do with working around the house and looking after Kamlesh. One day, I saw her trying to hold the pen in her hand and draw the line. When she saw me, she said she couldn't do it. I showed her how to hold a pen in her hand and she drew a big zig-zag line. All I wanted was for her to remember the straight-line number one on the bus that went to the south side instead of catching the wrong bus, and she was quite sure that she understood.

We had a very friendly talk and agreed that I could work Saturday overtime so we would have more money and she could catch the bus by herself and do the shopping. Reluctantly she agreed. I took her to the bus stop and pretended to catch another bus to go somewhere else. She got on bus number one, but I was afraid she would get off at the wrong stop although I'd given her instructions for where to get off the bus. I wrote our address and the shop address on pieces of paper and put them in her different pockets so if she lost one, she'd have another one to guide her. I just couldn't resist, and I caught another bus to follow her. I saw her on the road with a paper in her hand inquiring about the shop from a suitable person. I jumped off at the next stop and took her to the right shop. Although she'd gotten off at the wrong stop, it gave me a lot of confidence that she could handle the situation. So, she got lost a couple of times, but managed to find the shop with the help of the paper. I was amazed at the energy and vitality she showed.

One day an old Scottish lady knocked on my door. When I opened it, the old lady said, "I brought a gift for you." I didn't know her or what she was talking about, and then she laughingly said, "I brought your wife home, as she was lost." I thanked the lady. Nasib Kaur had gotten off the bus a couple of stops early and given the paper with the address to the old lady. The old lady had walked with her to the house.

The important thing was that she'd managed to get out of the house and struggle to get on and off the bus at the right places to buy the food independently. It took a few months of courage for her do the shopping independently, which was a big help for me. She saw clearly that I was working more overtime and bringing home more money to spend. I wanted to put my confidence in, and I was able to. We were alone, and the main thing was to keep ourselves happy. I didn't push her to do anything, but she was learning enough to do things on her own. I was happy that the same simple person with no education, born in a tiny village, who had never had a chance to move freely outside her village, was now moving through the busy streets of Glasgow responsibly and looking after her family independently. This was a great achievement for her and for me. It was a stunning victory for us, and I was almost intoxicated with the joy of it.

Mr. Wood, my coworker, invited us a few times to his house a few blocks away from our residence, but that wasn't enough as Mrs. Chand wasn't fluent in English. Then I took her a few times to Alexandra Parade Park, a beautiful park with lots of flowers and shrubs only half a mile from our home. She did go there off and on, but I was feeling more concerned than she was about her loneliness. I was afraid she would become sick. I bought a beautiful big radiogram that looked like a piece of furniture so she could play Indian music that she had brought from Delhi. My neighbor came to see the radiogram while I was out and helped her with the ins and outs of it.

In the meantime, we had another baby, Anil. She was born in August 1956 at Duke Street Hospital. The baby was born premature, and the first time I saw her, I was really scared. But thanks to the doctors and nurses, who treated my baby like their own, after a few months she was able to come home. She was beautiful and adorable with lots of hair on her head, and so delicate that I was afraid to touch her. My wife made sure that I washed my hands perfectly before I touched her. My daughter Kamlesh now had company to play with, and she became very fond of her sister. When the baby cried, she also started to cry. Now my wife had more responsibility that kept her busy. She had to do the shopping on Duke Street, just a five-minute walk from home. I bought a beautiful stroller for the baby so she could be independent and walk easily to the shops. I bought beautiful clothes from a Jew's shop on Candleriggs Street. My neighbors loved to see the baby, especially an old policeman, who was very friendly and warm and used to walk around the shopping area on Duke Street, loved baby Anil and often talked to her.

In 1956 and before, the UK was a very special country and people liked to know about how things were there, especially Mr. Shiv Raj. He used to write to us often, about every two to three weeks. Also, letters from my parents arrived regularly. My wife took special care of the mail and kept it in a box. I had to read each letter two or three times, until she was fully satisfied with every word of it. This inspired her to take on the responsibility of going to the post office to buy the airmail letter and post it. We always thanked Shiv Raj for his correspondence. In those days I was getting so much mail from India that I had hardly enough time to cope with it. People wanted to come to the UK and wanted me to provide letters of undertaking or other documents.

Although by this time we'd been married for nine or ten years and had two children, Nasib Kaur's downcast look made me realize she was shy. In India she was buried with ancient traditions and present misery. She had a habit of walking behind me and fixing her dopatta (head scarf) on her head all the time. She was a traditional woman and old Punjabi village traditions upset me greatly. I knew she was a stranger to the new country, but she wasn't in an Indian village anymore, and I didn't want a slave for a wife. I wanted her to be a sincere wife and an equally responsible partner. At first, I found this traditional mentality a very hard nut to crack, but she soon understood everything and changed her habits for the better. She appreciated that I was working hard during the day until four o'clock and attending evening classes at a local college afterward.

Within a year or so, she reluctantly took on all the responsibilities of the house and children. She progressed satisfactorily, but it was still far from enough. We both had very busy lives and I gave her more and more responsibilities. In the ensuing years, she managed to understand and learned to speak English with the help of our children and our good Scottish neighbors. By practicing she had picked up just enough English for conversational purposes that served her as she conducted all her business, whether it was dealing with a grocery store cashier, travel agent, or bank clerk independently. She baffled me sometimes, but I didn't have the problem of having a wife who was afraid or tried to run away from the situation. It was a great help in all the difficulties I confronted. We were deeply attached to each other. She was passionate about getting on in life and her life changed dramatically. She had tremendous willpower and a good mind of her own to tackle anything independently.

MY WIFE SUPPORTS MY STRUGGLE

It was a very painful and complicated decision for me to go to Northampton, away from home, to complete City and Guilds of London Institute courses, and later I went to Leather Sellers College in London, four hundred miles away, to do advanced studies. Nasib Kaur reluctantly agreed that I should go. She saw the greatness of our struggle and had a unique willingness to sacrifice herself for its continuation. She learned how to sign her name in English as well as in Urdu, learned to do basic transactions at the local bank, and became independent. She practiced writing her name in her leisure time at least twice a week. Any success I had in my studies was because I had her behind me and at my side, a devoted, understanding, dedicated, and patient companion. She wrote asking Shiv Raj to send her clothes and spent money very wisely on our household because we didn't have any income during those two years. Although I did my best as her husband and the father of our young children to fly home from London every weekend, she was fully responsible and in charge of all the household and childcare tasks. She took the children to the hospital when they were sick and nursed them at home.

One of our daughters broke her arm, and she took her to a hospital far away and managed to nurse her back to health beautifully. She bought food and paid the bills on time. During these most tragic experiences, she never became overemotional or panicky. Many good ideas came to her through her own acts as she was self-made person. She always had stories to tell me when I arrived home from London every weekend after midnight. These responsibilities gave new meaning to her life and changed her world.

After my college education, I'd worked hard and moved from one place to another to better myself. I moved from one country to another in search of true freedom. I endured a lot of hardships and frustration in an unending struggle. She brought me comfort and solace when I needed it the most and she continued to support me for our family's good.

OUR ACCOMMODATIONS

In Glasgow, we lived in an old but very good residential area among Scottish people with full freedom and far from the dogmatism of Indian and Pakistani society, where my wife and children had a good chance to grow without the diseases of caste and prejudice. Our Scottish neighbors treated us with love and respect and were helpful and useful. In return, we were very grateful and generous and invited them and their children to make friends with our own children, to the extent that some of them even developed a habit of eating curry and chapati from our house. We couldn't help being grateful to people who were interested in us. It was fun to have them around. We saw a godly spirit in their behavior and eyes, and we had a carefree life. My wife's simplicity and her straight and plain aesthetic manner carved a place in everyone's heart. She was a humble person and kept a low profile all her life. Her objective was not to deprive but to provide, a virtue she learned from my father. She loved and helped everybody, so everyone liked her, and we led an independent life with dignity and respect. My good neighbors often mentioned to me that even though she didn't have a college degree, she had deep reservoir, of common sense, a great virtue.

NASIB KAUR'S COMFORT ZONE

My wife had refined taste in everything, but she wasn't a big spender and she knew how to economize. She bought durable clothes for our children from the fashionable and reasonably priced Marks Spencer Store in Glasgow and never went to cheap Indian or Pakistani stores. She loved good food and never hesitated to spend money on fresh fruit and vegetables. Now and then, when she was in the mood, she took me to her favorite Italian ice cream shop to spend an evening together. She was very fond of gold but was never willing to wear cheap trinkets or anything less than pure twenty-four-carat gold.

I must admit I was bossy and stubborn in my attempts to change her old Indian habits and traditions when she first came to Scotland. She had initially refused to understand, to spend Scottish money or take any responsibility, but she was well versed in these things now and I let her enjoy her life freely and without too much fuss and interruption. I tried to be fair to her and she could buy and sell anything. Her favorite pastime was to go to the theater and enjoy a good Indian movie. She saw Mother India movies many times because she was also a victim of similar circumstances and these movies were a great inspiration to her. She also became very interested in Lata and Rafi songs and always reminded me about the program on radio or television. Since she was living far away from the Indian community and I never allowed her to mix too much with any family, she spent a lot of time calling her dear and near ones in India and England and enjoyed life to the fullest with her children and husband.

A GOOD CAREGIVER

My wife took great care of the health and welfare of our children. In 1969, she was invited with her two youngest daughters to serve as a Dennistoun district representative by the lord provost of Glasgow to take part in launching the city's polio vaccination scheme at the Glasgow City Chambers. Our daughter Rajrani, age three, born in 1966, was the first to be vaccinated by the lord provost for the program's inauguration. My wife nearly declined the invitation because I wasn't home, and she asked our good neighbor to phone me in London for permission. She was deeply devoted to her children and was always willing to sacrifice her own needs for theirs. She refrained from visiting her family in India for sixteen years because she thought her young children would suffer in her absence. She was instrumental in educating all seven of our adorable daughters to the master's, bachelor's degree levels and other levels at top American universities. She had only one agenda, which was to give her daughters the best and highest education, and for that she was happy to sacrifice her own life. She wanted to protect her daughters from the misery and hardship she had gone through and made sure that her all daughters become self-sufficient and independent and lived with dignity and respect. She was so happy and proud that she'd managed to make her dream come true. She put up an unyielding struggle and her hard work paid off.

Top: My Wife and I in Scotland (1958)
Bottom: My Second Job with the Glasgow Corporation of Transport (1956)

CHAPTER TWENTY FIVE

EDUCATION & TRAINING IN SCOTLAND

During my employment with Miller Tanning Company in September 1954, I became very interested in learning more about the process of leather-making. In theory, it was much the same as what was done in my father's company in India. One day the work manager saw me looking at things during my lunch break and said that if I was interested in learning, I could go to the local college. In fact, he was teaching leather manufacturing there. Tuition was nearly free tuition, and classes were held in the evening. I was alone then, a newcomer from India without any real friendship or company, and it was hard to pass the evenings during the long days of summer. It was a real opportunity to pass the time and do something worthwhile. I was a little late, but I was admitted to evening courses at David Dale College in the Bridgeton area of Glasgow, about one mile from my house. Attending college in the evening and working full time during the day kept me busy and out of any mischief. It was a good start and great hopes grew within me.

In 1955, I passed my preliminary examination at the City and Guilds of London Institute. I attended this college from 1954 to 1957, passing the preliminary, intermediate, and other stages, but I got stuck in the final year as classes were discontinued because there were only three students left. I didn't know what to do. Finally, I learned that there were a couple of other colleges in England where I could finish the courses by attending full-time or evening classes. But I was in no mood to go to England, leaving my wife and children in Glasgow, Scotland. My wife gave birth to our third baby girl in October 1957, and one of our friends named her Shukesh.

COLLEGE IN NORTHAMPTON: 1959

I didn't let the opportunity pass and decided to attend evening classes at Strathclyde University on Duke Street near the city center, studying business management in 1958. After a year, I passed Accounting and Business Law, but I wasn't happy as my mind was focused on finishing the leather-making courses. I made inquiries and wrote a letter to the Northampton College of Technology. The head of the leather department was kind enough to give me all the related information and promised to find suitable employment for me among the many tanneries in Northampton if I needed employment. The tuition was reasonable, and I could afford it. I checked my bank balance and made plans to go to Northampton. I didn't want to be away from my family, but the appetite to finish the courses became stronger.

Finding employment in Northampton and attending classes in the evening was a long and tedious process. I decided to attend full-time day courses and the head of the department gladly accepted me in 1959. I worked hard during the week and did my best to travel home to

Glasgow on the weekends, but it was too difficult as there were no direct trains to and from Northampton.

In Northampton, I stayed in the house of Mrs. Noga on Charles Street. She was from Poland and had a big house. The other rooms were occupied by a Muslim named Mohammed Ifthkar from Pakistan and a Brahman from India named Sharma Bhushan Trikka. Here, for the first time in my life, I had a chance to meet and live with a Muslim and a Brahman as an untouchable. Mr. Trikka was the one who introduced me to Mrs. Noga. I was traveling from Coventry to Northampton and Mr. Trikka was on the same early morning train from Birmingham.

The train wasn't busy, and I sat behind him. He saw me and introduced himself to me. I told him that I had enrolled in college and had to arrange lodging. He gave me his address and asked me to visit him if I couldn't find a suitable place. I went to the college and the office gave me the address of a Bengali woman from India for board and lodging. I visited her and she had a very big room on the second floor, with four or five beds like what was normal India, all in a row. I peeked into the room and immediately walked out. I went to Charles Street through the park. Here Mr. Trikka talked to Mrs. Noga and she gladly gave me a room to rent.

In the evening I met Mr. Ifthkar (the Pakistani). I must say they were good people and I, for the first time, enjoyed the company of a Muslim and a Brahman, which changed my opinion that there were no good Muslims or Brahmans. Trikka was working full time, but by Wednesday or Thursday all his money was spent on drinking, smoking, and rent. Every Thursday, he asked me for a loan of two or three pounds and he returned the money on Saturday or Sunday. I always teased him by saying he was a very good Brahman.

He liked to offer me cigarettes for company's sake, but I was a nonsmoker and always refused. One Saturday, Mr. Trikka and Mr. Ifthkar were drunk, and they came home late. They offered me a cigarette and a drink, but I refused. Then they held me down on the floor and put a cigarette in my mouth. I had no escape and just agreed to smoke it if they didn't force me. So that was the start of my cigarette smoking, but I wasn't happy about it. I joined them, but I never bought cigarettes while in Northampton. I became addicted to cigarettes and I was drifting toward my doom. In the next ten years, I made holes in a half dozen pairs of pants while smoking and driving. Later, when I bought a house in New Jersey, I laid new maroon carpet throughout the house. My children were worried that I would burn the carpet, so they put ashtrays in each room and hung posters of cigarette damage to the lungs. They were watching me all the time. I was so fed up that I decided to give up smoking, and so I did.

Mr. Ifthkar was poor and thrifty, and I think he saved as much money as he could. He always admired my clothes because all my suits were custom-made. I wore expensive shirts. Mrs. Noga thought very highly of me because I always paid the rent in advance or on time and never caused any problems for her. I had a habit of treating women with respect. I joked with her and her husband quite a lot when they were alone, but in other people's company, I treated them with respect. In fact, she thought I was a very rich man. I was actually very poor, but my habits and character were rich. Mrs. Noga taught me the importance of eating on time and helped me gain weight.

From Glasgow I used to catch the evening train for Birmingham, and from Birmingham I changed trains for Northampton so I could get to college on time. Winter lasts longer in England, and it was quite cold in March. One day I met a person of Indian or Pakistani origin. He was standing in Northampton Square, wearing only a light overcoat and shivering with cold. I saw him from the top of the double-decker bus, and as I got out, I said good morning to this stranger, picked up his small bag, and asked him to come with me. He didn't ask any questions and came along with me to Charles Street where I was residing, half a mile from the town center.

After coffee we talked about the weather. Then I gave him cornflakes with milk. He took it gladly without any hesitation or questions. To me, he was just another poor Indian or Pakistani as I once was when I was new to the country. He was a human being too, and I wasn't concerned with his color or creed. I changed the bedsheets, showed him to my bed, and asked him to rest and sleep. He slept for a few hours, then came back downstairs and I gave him lunch with coffee. After finishing lunch, he asked me why I hadn't asked any questions about who he was. I replied that to me, he was just another human being like me, and we need each other's help in times of need. He was educated and had a BA degree. He was impressed with my talk and behavior. His name was Sahibzada Mir Feroze Ali Khan and he was from Hyderabad, India. I became suspicious and wondered why he was calling himself Sahibzada but standing in a square at a bus stop in the shivering cold. I left this question for later. He'd come to study boot- and shoemaking and I viewed this as just an excuse to get out of India. He gave up his studies after three or four months and started a full-time job at a laundry service, pressing clothes. He was a well-mannered and religious person. He asked me if he could live there, so I asked Mrs. Noga to give him an empty room. Later I found that when he wanted to pray, he always waited for me to go away to my bedroom. Soon, Mrs. Noga found out that he was using hot water to wash his backside in the toilet rather than using toilet paper, which was wetting the bathroom floor. Plus, he was using extra electricity for light and to heat water. She talked to me about it, but I didn't want to get involved in religious matters. Finally, she asked him to leave as he didn't want to change his habits. He told me he was one of the many children of Nawab of Hyderabad. That was why he was called Sahibzada, because he was legally a prince. I just settled on calling him Ali Khan. Later he visited me in Glasgow, and I showed him around.

During my course of study as a full-time student, I found it very difficult to understand the professor's dialect when he was lecturing. He was from Yorkshire and his accent was totally different from those in the rest of the country. I was always worried about how I would get through the examinations as my notebook contained so many blank lines and missing words. I was timid and didn't want to become a nuisance in the class by accusing him of not speaking correctly. One day in the evening, I was working late on my practical, and Mr. Sharphouse, the head of the department, met me. We were alone and he asked me why I always looked sad. Was there a problem at home, or anything he could help with? He was very sincere and polite. I'd never met anyone so sincere in my life. He had a profound influence on me. He was my professor and not a stranger, so I told him frankly that I had a wife and children, but they weren't any worry for me. I'd calculated everything before attending and I went home now and then to see my family. Then I explained that I hadn't been able to understand Mr. Jones's lectures and I was worried about passing my exams.

He started laughing and said, "Don't we all have trouble with his talk!" He advised me to keep myself happy and leave the exams to him. He would make sure that I made it through the examination successfully. He advised me to buy at least the previous five years' questions and he gave me the address to request them. He made it my responsibility to find the answers to the questions from the library books and college notes. After I filled in the answers, he wanted me to leave the papers on his desk. He would check them and return them to me. I was very happy. I ordered the questions and started spending my evenings in the local library, studying day and night. I became very engrossed and worked hard. The same year, in February 1960, we were blessed with another addition to our family. My wife gave birth to a baby and we named her Raksha Devi, the fourth child.

At the end I think I was the only student who passed all the exams. Mr. Sharphouse was very happy, and he congratulated me. He wrote to my previous employers regarding my extensive experience in the leather industry. After a few months, I was awarded a full technological certificate in leather dyeing and finishing. Mr. Sharphouse was key to this turning point in my life, and I owe him so much gratitude. Without his kind help, I don't think I would have passed the exams, let alone have gotten the full technological certificate in 1961. He was really an inspiration to me.

ADMISSION FOR MY YOUNGER BROTHER

The same day, out of the blue, an idea entered my mind. I was very frank with Mr. Sharphouse and I was very well known to Mr. Thronton, the head of the boot and shoe department. In the morning, I went to college to say goodbye to the teachers, and I hoped to see Mr. Sharphouse in private to have a chat with him. He was a well-wisher, kind in personal relations, and always wanted his students to grow. During our conversation, I mentioned to him that it would be good if I had more knowledge about boot and shoe manufacturing.

He abruptly said, "Let's go to Mr. Thronton and see what he says."

Then I said, "I'm thinking of bringing my younger brother into the boot and shoe manufacturing program. He's attending college in India. If I get his admission papers, he can come and take courses next year."

Mr. Thronton gave me the letter of admission, and I thanked him. I was very happy.

But at that time, I didn't know that I was digging my own grave and my own brother would prove to be a backstabber. My brotherly love clouded my mind and blinded my eyes. I was determined to make his life better and to see if his eyes could be cured here, like Nasib Kaur's. The feeling that he might prove useful to the community at large and better himself made me go to the teacher to seek his admission so I could bring him to the UK. There was nothing wrong with loving and helping my brother, but it didn't turn out as I hoped. One thing led to another, and it finally caused the destruction of the whole family. I was thoroughly committed to helping my brother any way I could, and at that time, I didn't know what the future would hold.

So, saying goodbye to Mrs. Noga and my friends, I left Charles Street and boarded the train to Birmingham, then to Glasgow. I was very proud and confident that I would get a suitable job in the leather industry in Glasgow, but unfortunately there were a few tanneries there, and I didn't find a job where I could use my education.

BACK TO THE GLASGOW CORPORATION

I ended up working for the Glasgow Corporation as a bus conductor again, which paid more than a leather industry job, but I wasn't happy. In those days, it was relatively easy to get a job as a bus conductor or driver with the Glasgow Corporation as an educated Indian or Pakistani. The reason was that people from India and Pakistan were hungry for money and jobs and willing to work hard compared to Scottish people. Scottish people were very angry that foreigners from India or Pakistan could show up and start with the corporation within a week or less. The local media turned against the corporation, saying that there was a shortage of work for locals and the corporation was giving the jobs away to Indians or Pakistanis.

In a TV interview, a corporation official offered the defense that the company wasn't concerned about whether new hires were Scottish, Indian, or Pakistani. They were concerned only with honesty on the job. Again, the media turned against the corporation, accusing them of insulting local workers and producing evidence of Indian and Pakistani workers collecting fares from customers that were nearly double those collected by Scottish workers. The media claimed the corporation preferred Indian and Pakistani conductors because by hiring locals, they would lose a lot of money. The corporation was right that we Indians were much more educated than the Scottish workers, and even the inspectors. We didn't want a Scottish inspector to tell us off or report us; we felt such an insult and a dishonor outweighed the benefits of the job. Therefore, we made sure that all fares were collected at the terminal before the bus moved. This made the job a lot easier, whereas the Scottish conductors took breaks or smoked at the terminal, so they overlooked a lot of fare collections during peak hours.

Top: My wife with my children (1958)
Bottom Left: 1960
Bottom Right: My Wife and I (1962)

CHAPTER TWENTY SIX

CHAREN GINDA
1959

My father always taught me to pass along my success, knowledge, and wisdom to those less fortunate. One example of this was the story of a promising, handsome boy named Charen Ginda. He had natural instincts and used to play football in my big backyard after school hours all by himself. He hardly talked much to anyone. He was a distant grandnephew of mine; his great grandfather and my grandfather were brothers. His mother died when he was very young. His father was in the army of lower rank soldiers, and his auntie was raising him alongside her own children.

One evening when I was in Scotland, a friend, Jagar Singh of Cobourg Street, Glasgow, met me and inquired whether I knew Charen Ginda. Jagar Singh was a Jat Sikh from Nakodar and had been living in Glasgow for a long time. He received a letter from his nephews in India about their high school results. My grandnephew Charen Ginda was ranked first, not only in school but in the Nakodar *tehsil*, and second in the district. When Jagar Singh told me this news, he said jokingly that an untouchable couldn't do that. I was thrilled to hear about it, and it was a matter of great pride for me and for my village and the community. With a full heart and great pride, I sent a beautiful congratulatory card to Charen Ginda.

On the weekend, I met Jagar Singh in a clothing warehouse owned by an orthodox Pakistani/Muslim haji named Faquir Muhammad. Jagar Singh joked with me that his two nephews were in the same class and were very bright students, but an untouchable chamar had beat them badly. He was in a lighthearted mood and we often joked with each other. I quipped thoughtlessly that he was a real untouchable champion, and nobody could touch or beat him in studies. He had dealt a big blow to the arrogance of those who held that education, and such attainments were only for high-caste Hindus, Sikhs, and Muslims.

The orthodox Muslim shopkeeper raged and fumed and sneered in fury and started cursing untouchables. He was outraged, really burnt up. He simply couldn't endure my speech. He could have politely asked me to leave, but power and prejudice had intoxicated him to an inordinate extent. I left the shop immediately without listening to any further insults. It just showed how these people, whether Muslim, Sikh, or Hindu, couldn't bear it if a chamar occasionally excelled and outshone them.

Charen Ginda won the scholarship and enrolled at DAV College in Jalandhar for further studies. Since he was a bright student, I was very optimistic about him and he was always on my mind. Near the end of his final year in college, I wrote to him asking what he intended to do after getting his degree. I was studying in England that year, 1959. He responded that he would get a job in Delhi in one of the government offices like many of his community members, and his parents were already looking for a suitable young woman for him to marry.

I knew he wasn't aware of his surroundings and what was happening in India. Nehru's government had a plan to build seven technical institutes, and the second had just opened in Bombay. Instinctively, I wrote to ask what he thought about taking some engineering courses since a clerical job wasn't good enough for him. After getting my letter, he was energized. He immediately went to Bombay and sent me a telegram asking for eight hundred rupees for his admission fee. I was already out of a job, but I wanted to help him, so I sent the money by telegram to his friends' address. He was getting a scholarship of a hundred rupees a month, and I promised I would pay his extra dues for the next four or five years.

He wrote to me every month and we became very good friends. He successfully finished his degree in electrical engineering at the Indian Institute of Technology and was designated a pilot officer in the Indian air force. After settling down in a job, he wrote to me about his marriage. He wanted a nice educated girl from the same community. He told me time and again that he had two college degrees now and he deserved to be married to a decent girl with at least one degree. In the 1960s, well-educated girls were scarce in my community, and they weren't enthusiastic about the nature of his employment. As a pilot officer, he would fly planes, which was a very dangerous job. They didn't know that it was only the name of a rank. However, he had no luck and a year passed in frustration. Finally, he wrote asking my opinion about marrying a Malhotra Hindu girl outside his community. This girl liked him and belonged to an educated family and she was interested in marrying him. They knew each other and were colleagues. Against all odds, he married the Malhotra girl.

I visited Delhi three months after the wedding for a short while. She was alone in the apartment in Rajokri, New Delhi. I introduced myself, and she was very happy to receive me. I was surprised that within only a few months of the wedding, she already had a plan to buy a plot of land and build a house. After a year or so, I got a letter and I helped them with a small amount of money, which was returned to me after a year. They bought a plot of land in Gurgaon, Haryana, near Delhi, and built a house. They used part of the house as a residence and the other as a school for children. She tutored children on the weekends and after work hours. They settled down nicely, and after that, I didn't hear much from them for years. I was very annoyed, but that wasn't new to me and I wished them well. Many times, I waited for a New Year's card from them and I didn't know their address as they moved often. Whenever I visited India, I asked their family about their well-being.

Charen Ginda was very enthusiastic. He gained many qualifications through further studies and was promoted to ever higher ranks, like flying officer and then squadron leader. Finally, he retired from the Air Force after serving for twenty-six years at the rank of wing commander. He retired at the age of fifty-eight and he was worried about what to do next.

I was living in the US by this time. Eventually, he wrote to me with an impressive resume so I could arrange a job for him in the US as he was still young and didn't want to remain idle. He had a good chance, so I contacted some big companies and they liked his resume. His wife and children were well settled in India. I knew from previous experience that people liked to come to the US, but then didn't want to go back to their families, and that bothered me a great deal. Considering all the odds and ends, I was forced to tell him that it was hard to find employment in the US and that he should stay with his family in India. He had two children: a son who was employed at an oil company in India and later emigrated to Canada, and a daughter who became a doctor after earning her MBBS. His son earned an MBA from Western University in Canada and worked for IBM before joining Shell Oil Company as a manager. Back home, Charen Ginda and his wife bought four to five acres of land in a poor area of Gurgaon and opened a school there for students up to tenth grade.

The last time I visited them, they took me to the school. I was impressed with its success, but she was in a poor state of health. She wanted to extend the school to twelfth grade and was asking for my help. I had my own problems putting my children and grandchildren through university, plus I needed money for retirement as medical bills are so expensive. Later she died at the age of seventy-one, which was a big shock to the children, to Charen Ginda, and to me. However, they had established themselves well with hard work, wisdom, and ingenuity, and they were out of the woods. Hard work and my little bit of timely help paid off, and I am just blessed and proud to be a small part of this success story and happy that they appreciate and remember me as a part of it.

CHAPTER TWENTY SEVEN

MY RETURN VISIT TO INDIA
AUGUST 1962

I had secured my admission, and it was my dream to go to the National Leather Sellers College in London to start a diploma or an associate degree course in September 1962. It had been eight years since I left India and I hadn't seen my mother and father. I was very homesick and often became emotional, asking myself a lot of questions and wondering why I hadn't gone to visit them. Sometimes I cried. I didn't have enough money to pay for my studies and cover my brother's expenses. I decided to go to India with the excuse that the next two years would be tough while I was attending college and I would have no other chance to see my parents. Without consulting my wife, I booked a one-way ticket to India via Karachi, Pakistan. I didn't even notify my parents. There were no telephones then, and a postcard would have taken at least a few days to reach them.

After arriving at Delhi Airport, I took the Sardar Ji (Sikh) taxi service to Moti Bagh in Delhi, where my brother-in-law Shiv Raj lived. The driver stopped the taxi on the main road and pointed out the house to me. I gave him a big note for fare. I had no small notes for the exact fare. He took the note from me, telling me that he would get the change from a nearby shop. He started the taxi, drove away with the big note, and never returned. This was a bad omen and a prediction of Sardar Ji's behavior.

My brother-in-law was very surprised to see me, especially in my best suit, well fed, and looking handsome. Before he welcomed me in, his first reaction was that he should get ready and go to the UK. I stayed with him for one night and asked him to put me on the first-class train to Punjab. Instead, he put me on an ordinary train from Delhi. We went to the station a little early and boarded the train. All the seats were empty. Shiv Raj put me in a compartment with six passenger seats. I spread a foreign-made towel on my seat and started reading a *Time* magazine I'd bought in London. It was an early morning train, especially for college students. I saw students and other passengers boarding the train, but no one came into my compartment.

I was surprised and wondered if they thought the compartment was reserved or felt awkward or shy about sitting beside a well-dressed passenger. Passengers were standing in the corridor, but no one came into my compartment to occupy the empty seats. The train moved on, and I was rather amused that eight years before, people hadn't liked sitting near me because I was a low-class untouchable. Now, they wouldn't sit beside me because I was better dressed than they were, and they might have felt that they were of a lower class than me.

After a few hours, an army officer with a lot of badges boarded the train at Ambala Cantt and came into my compartment. I was lying on the seat and tried to sit up. He told me gently to keep lying and no one would bother me. He was right; no one came near me. In Ludhiana he helped me get off the train. I changed trains for Nakodar and arrived there in the evening.

At the train station, I spotted a person in red coolie clothes. I shouted to him, but he didn't come. Finally, a fellow passenger saw me shouting and brought him to me. He looked terrified. I asked him twice whether he recognized me, but he didn't answer. He picked up both suitcases and headed toward Dana Mandi, and I shouted that I didn't want to go that way. I wanted to go the opposite way, to a nearby colony. He was perplexed, and after a while he asked me which house I wanted to go to. I said that I didn't want to tell him as he knew the house. He had been to my house many times before I moved to the UK.

I told him not to run since I wasn't in a hurry and said, "Look at me and recognize me."

He was still puzzled. I told him I was the same person he had helped when I was admitted to the local hospital ten years before.

He was happy and ran with the suitcases to my house to give the news of my arrival to my parents. He met my *bhabhi*, Jai Rani, outside the house and without waiting for me, she rushed to my parents. They came to see me at the main gate. My mother started crying. My father was also very emotional and hugged me. I must say, I was a changed man, not as shy as before, full of truth, experienced, and above all, in the best health they had seen me in since I was a boy. My mother never let me out of her sight. She always looked at my hands, which were soft and gentle. She kissed my hands every time I went near her. My father was very happy and proud of me. One day he looked at my hands and asked me why they were so nice and soft. He had seen hands full of blisters and hard as rocks on other people who'd visited him from the UK. I told him that most of the time, I did light jobs that I could handle easily.

My father's friends and relatives invited me for dinner, but I told him not to accept any invitations and to say that I was sick.

My father didn't want to lie, and he was a little annoyed. At one point he asked, "Why don't you like my village's people anymore?"

I explained to him that I didn't drink alcohol and there was a chance of getting sick by drinking homemade liquor. I couldn't afford to get sick and I had to go back to my wife and children. My father understood my reasons and complimented me for keeping away from alcohol and drunkards. He was very happy that I was in good health and looking after my wife and children. When I was young, they had tried their best to keep me healthy, but I was always sick and underweight, and they worried about me all the time. My father was thankful that I had come back to see them and show them my good health, and their worries were over. I talked to my father heart to heart. He understood me better than anybody else.

There were whispers in the neighborhood about how much money I'd brought home from the UK, and these whispers reached my parents' ears. My father told the neighbors that his son was in good health and was a good person and that was everything he'd ever wanted. I told my father that what I gained from going to the UK was my health and my wife's health, plus education and my own home to live in. To my father, this was more than enough achievement. He was satisfied that I could look after myself and my family.

As the days passed, I started thinking about booking my passage back to Glasgow. I told my father I needed to go to Delhi to make the arrangements. He didn't want to part with me and told me that he would send for a booking agent to come to the house. In the meantime, I got a letter from a friend in Glasgow, Lali Ram, asking me to bring his three children to the UK. So, the travel agent came and took our names and told us to meet him in New Delhi to get tickets and pay for them there. I went to Delhi with the other passengers and met the agent in a hotel called the Ambassador to collect the tickets.

There was a travel agency there. The agent asked us to sit in the lobby of the hotel and collected money from us, then went to the travel agency clerk and quietly disappeared. We waited for half an hour, but he was nowhere to be seen. We inquired of the travel company and they refused to talk to us. They didn't know the man. We lost a good amount of money in the blink of an eye. I was disappointed and stayed overnight with Shiv Raj. Somehow my father learned about this incident and sent my younger brother to bring me back home. The next day I received a letter stating that my wife had given birth to a beautiful child. I was a little upset, and I'll never forget my agony of conscience for not being there with my wife in her difficult hours. She named our baby Kamala, the name of a flower.

After spending a few more days at my parents'

home, I wrote to my wife to book my seat to Scotland, and I flew back to Glasgow. But before I left India, another incident happened. I had to apply to the Reserve Bank of India for permission to take some money out of the country. When I was in Delhi to accomplish this, my friend Gorman Chand and I went to the India gate and sat on the grassy lawn to pass the time before returning to the Reserve Bank. When we went back, we realized we'd left the envelope containing all our documents on the lawn where we were sitting. I was very disheartened that I'd lost the documents and now I couldn't apply for foreign exchange. After two days, I received a telegram from a gentleman in Delhi saying that he'd found an envelope and I could get it from him. He gave me the full address to reach him. I took the train to Delhi and retrieved the documents. I thanked him and tried to take him to lunch, but he refused. Instead, he served me coffee and cookies in his office. It was reassuring to see that there are some good people in India.

LEGAL CHANGES

While I was in India, I noted that some laws had changed. People reading English papers told me I must apply to the British High Commission office to get a new visa. I went to Delhi and Shiv Raj sent his friends with me to the British embassy. There was a big Pashtun at the gate. He stopped me and my friends from entering. I listened to my friends and brother-in-law, who were telling me to get a new visa to the UK and other nonsense, but I was frustrated. Then one day I hired a taxi myself and went to the embassy. The gatekeeper asked for my passport. I showed him my Indian passport and again he told me that I couldn't go in. While I was talking to him, an English embassy officer was exiting through the gate.

I was so frustrated, and I shouted to him, "Sir, stop for a second! I have a passport and have lived in the UK for the past eight years and this gatekeeper is not letting me in."

He quickly checked my passport and told me to get it stamped.

I explained to him that I had been running back and forth for the last three days. I said, "I'm very frustrated with your Indian employee. If you don't mind, could you do it for me?"

He was good enough to go back in with my passport, get it stamped, and return it to me within a few minutes. The next day, I flew back to Scotland.

CHAPTER TWENTY EIGHT

(The National College for Leather Industry)
THE NATIONAL LEATHER SELLERS COLLEGE
LONDON: 1962

While in India, I planned to come back to Glasgow before long and prepare for college in London. But I was overcome by lassitude and overwhelming problems there, which delayed my return. It was imperative that I get to college on time and not miss any lectures, but I was late. I landed in London the day I was supposed to start. The mental anguish of living away from my wife and children and being late to college was the worst I had ever suffered.

Nonetheless, I took the plane from London to Glasgow. After spending a few days there with my family, I flew back to London to start college. I had to arrange for lodging, and I knew a few friends in London. I visited them that Saturday, but they were living far outside of London. Then I learned about a friend who was living on the east side, about fifteen miles from the college on Tower Bridge Road. He had a house and was glad to rent a room to me. The National Leather Sellers College was the nation's educational institution for the leather industry, a small private college specializing in advanced leather science and technology and preparing students for the leather trade. It was very well equipped with analytical laboratories and a model tanning yard for practice. The college had a rich history and many scientists and technologists of repute had attended there. It was a fine college with great possibilities.

I felt bad because I was at least a week late. I met Dr. Danby, the principal of the college. After welcoming me, he called Dr. Sykes, the head of the science department and secretary of the college. They talked between themselves for a few minutes. To my surprise, the duration of the diploma courses had been increased to three years instead of the usual two years. I thought fees were £500 per year, but they'd been decreased to £250 per year. Dr. Danby discussed my course of study with me. I was hoping to finish the course of study in one year because I had already gained full technological certificates from the City and Guilds of London Institute. But Dr. Danby didn't think it was possible for me to cover everything in one year. I received a list of required courses, and I was shocked to learn how many there were, some of which I had never even heard of. Dr. Danby advised me to start a two-year course of study and see how everything went.

However, I started attending classes in the middle of September in 1962. I'd forgotten most of what I studied in Northampton because of the two-year gap. Dr. Sykes was a scientist with a good reputation in the leather industry. He expected me to know a lot. I was weak in sciences. However, I had to face the music. He was tough and gave me a hard time. For the other subjects, I wasn't worried as I had a good foundation of knowledge. I had to workday and night and managed to pass my second year, but then I learned that I would be given a college diploma if I finished my prescribed courses. This news eased the tension a little as I was sure to get the diploma.

In my third year, much of the emphasis was on project work. I was glad that I'd passed my second year despite all the difficulties I faced. My wife and children were living four hundred miles away in Glasgow, and I had the primary responsibility of putting food on the table for them. I was going through a very laborious time. Often, I shouted for God's help because there was no one else around and he was helping me in his mysterious ways. I love my family very much, and I wasn't prepared to desert them. I wanted to see them every weekend. This was very important to me, and to them. No matter how much I had to sacrifice, I made a point to see them every weekend, and God willing, I managed to do that.

After my first week in London, I went to Heathrow Airport. I was late, but the last flight was at 10:00 p.m. and I tried to catch it. I gave a £10 note to the booking lady and she gave me £7.50 in change. I thought she'd made a mistake and asked her if she knew she gave me too much money back. She said it wasn't a mistake. British Airways had introduced a standby fare, and the price was £2.50. The last half an hour of booking was sold at that price provided the seats were available. I was thrilled because that was cheaper than a coach fare to Glasgow. I thanked God for listening to my prayers. So, for two years, I commuted by plane between London and Glasgow. I never missed the 10:00 p.m. flight and I was on the plane to Glasgow every Friday evening.

My neighbors and friends thought I was wealthy, but I was very hard up. I had applied to the Reserve

Bank of India to transfer some money from India. But I didn't get any response from the Reserve Bank, or from home. I talked to my father, and he gave me the names of a few people in England and told me to get money from them because they owed him. I wasted time meeting with them, and they totally refused. I was frustrated and went to the Indian High Commission office in London. They wired the Reserve Bank in India, and I learned that the money had been sanctioned and a reply had been sent to my home in India. My father was not aware of having received any mail from the Reserve Bank. He asked my older brother, Shenker Dutt, and learned that he had received the Reserve Bank's reply but hadn't told my father. My father was quite annoyed at this and sent money without any further delay. What pained me the most in those days was my brother's behavior; it seemed he had lost touch with reality. This underhandedness shook me greatly and changed my whole outlook on life. He was a vigorous critic of my life decisions and his actions filled me with distaste.

After a few months, my younger brother Bhaj Ram got a job in London after finishing college. We stayed together for a few months until I finished my own courses, and he helped pay the rent and other expenses. In Glasgow, my wife needed clothes and she wrote a letter to her cousin's brother, Shiv Raj, in Delhi. He sent a few suits with someone coming to the UK. She cut down on extra expenses and tried to live on the bare minimum of food. Mrs. McDevitt, her daughter Mary and our other good neighbors kept her company when she was alone. In short, it was a life without beauty. It was mere subsistence, cold, cruel, and degenerative for me and for my family.

AN ONWARD JOURNEY

My work at college progressed very well. Both Dr. Danby and Mr. Humphreys were impressed. I completed my coursework and began writing my thesis.

God was listening to my prayers and good news came through Dr. Danby that one of his friends was moving to Scotland from Leeds. The man had bought an old building outside Glasgow and was looking for an experienced person to run the finishing department, and Dr. Danby had recommended me. The man was coming to meet me, but he had no time to wait as he was busy, and he had to return to Scotland. I was excited, almost intoxicated with joy over the news. After a couple of hours, Dr. Danby came to me while I was busy with my lab work, took me to his office, and introduced me to the owner of the company. The man told me that Dr. Danby had told him everything about me, about my home in Glasgow where my wife and children lived with me. He wanted someone to run his finishing department. He said I could start in one month or whenever I wanted. The pay wasn't very good as Dr. Danby told me the man was a miser, but I had to take it because I was desperate for a job and I accepted everything he said without any argument. Now I had a place to go and start work. I was thrilled, and I felt relaxed. I gave this news to my wife and she was very happy. I told my wife that my studies were over, I would be back soon, and the college would send my diploma by mail, but I didn't realize that I hadn't completed all the requirements. I thought that when the exam was over, I was free to go anywhere, as it had been at Northampton Technical College.

Mr. Humphreys gave me the shocking news that the following Friday, I would have to talk about my project in front of the students and teachers. I was dumbfounded and speechless. I turned pale and Mr. Humphreys asked what the problem was. He was my supervisor, and during my project of the previous four or five months, we'd become friends. I wasn't shy, and I very openly but reluctantly told him that I had never spoken before an audience, not even in front of my parents, never mind in public, and I was not a great talker.

He started laughing and said, "You've been talking to me quite a lot and making sense. You can talk in the hall in front of the public in the same way."

I said, "No, sir, you're different. I know you and you're a nice person."

He understood my difficulty and said that we would do something to make it easy. The next day he brought four dozen copies of my thesis, containing all my analytical work and testing results, and told me that before starting, I should give a copy to each person and let them read it. This would make it a lot easier for me and lessen the time I'd have to talk. It gave me a lot of courage, but I still struggled against my timidity. Friday came, and all the students and teachers were there. I appeared on time and I was always first because my name started with C. So, I started talking quite humbly, and used the word *we* instead of me. I was nervous and sweaty as I stood before the crowd.

As I talked further, I gained some confidence that I could handle it. Then, Dr. Sykes started asking questions: "This is your report, and you're a student. Who's the other guy?"

I said, "Sorry, sir, it's due to respect for my supervisor that I used the word *we*." I apologized, but I wasn't afraid of him anymore. He asked me a lot of technical questions, and I answered some of them with confidence. After all, it was my project and time was limited. A couple of times, I skipped things because the time was short. Finally, I thanked the teachers and students for putting up with me. The hard work was over, and I thanked Mr. Humphreys.

The following morning, a group of well-known personalities came to the college. I was again summoned by Dr. Danby to appear before them in his office. I talked to Mr. Humphres for advice and consultation. He told me that I shouldn't be afraid, that they would have my thesis, would introduce themselves to me and talk briefly to me. They were four scientists of very good reputation. I had seen Dr. Goldman visiting our college. The other man was a well-known personality, the head of the leather department at the University of Leeds, Dr. Burton, and the other two doctors, I didn't know. They were very pleasant indeed and asked me to feel at ease. They offered me coffee. It was a very friendly atmosphere. From them, I learned that Dr. Danby thought highly of my project.

"You've done very well in your project, and your work is going to be published in the Leather Trade Journal (Society of Leather Trades Chemists' Association)," said Dr. Goldman.

"The principal didn't tell me. I'm a student sir, and I'm doing the best I can to get my precious diploma," I replied.

They said, "We heard you have a job ready to go. Congratulations!" They asked me some questions about my project, which I answered easily, and it was all over.

I shook their hands and walked away.

Finally, the day came. We were taken to the Leather Sellers hall, somewhere in the middle of London. It was a beautiful hall; all the teachers and parents were there in their best clothes. The reception was fantastic. There was dinner and plenty to drink. I was the only one there alone because I didn't know about the graduation ceremony traditions. I could have brought my nephews from Wolverhampton. Anyhow, after the ceremony, my name was announced, and I was the first to get a diploma with honors. All the visitors congratulated me.

The next day was an all-day party. I was the oldest and married. My classmates came to me and said they would be happy if I joined them for a drink, but I wasn't in the mood. I wanted to go home. Officially, it wasn't over yet. They insisted, so I agreed. They fooled around all over the city, and I followed them. Then I did something bad. Mr. Tuck (a professor) invited us to a show in the evening. I went to Birmingham and turned late. It wasn't very nice of me and I regret this even today. The same evening, I left for Glasgow, and I started work the next morning with the Clyde Leather Company.

Top: My wife and my children (1963)
Bottom Left: North Hampton College of Technology (1960)
Bottom Right: 1964

CHAPTER TWENTY NINE

THE CLYDE LEATHER COMPANY
1964

After returning from London in June, 1964, I prepared to go to work the next morning. Neilston was far to the south of Glasgow. I had no car, so I had to take the train from Glasgow Central Station to Neilston, then walk about a quarter mile to the factory. The Clyde Leather Company factory was in an old three-story building and I wasn't very impressed by the sight. They must have bought it very cheap.

I met the chairman and owner, and he introduced me to his two sons, who were also graduates of Leeds University and National Leather Sellers College, a couple years ahead of me. They were much taller and younger than me. They took me to the main building, but there were no finishing machines or materials anywhere. They showed me an outdated, rusty spray unit and a few old drums of colors lying here and there and asked me to collect everything and make it work with the help of the maintenance man. However, within a week I was able to correct the spraying machine unit and cleaned the area for better working conditions.

I oversaw the finishing department, which involved color matching and mixing and preparing samples for customers. I had to do everything by weight so the color could be reproduced easily, and formulas could be developed for consistency. I had no experience, but my college professor had assured me that I would manage without much difficulty. The company was making suede from leather splits, byproducts of the leather industry. It was buying splits from other tanners in the country and selling the finished product to shoe and clothing manufacturers.

After a month on the job in Neilston, my nephew Harnam Dass and his wife came to see us from Wolverhampton. The same day, I received a letter from home written by Shenker Dutt asking me to send back money I'd received from my father. I was very upset that my father didn't trust me. I told Harnam Dass that I had to send £300 home and borrowed some money from him. Later, when I went home for another visit in India and showed anger toward my father for not trusting me to pay him back, he flatly denied knowing about the letter and said he'd never told my brother about the money. This meant that my brother wrote the letter without telling my father, and his behavior upset me a lot, but I couldn't show it.

The Railway Central Station was in the center of the town. It was surrounded by big stores. Every day I used to catch the city bus home from the bus stop in front of a store called Grant's, a home furnishing store. One day, I saw something new in the showroom and I went inside to find out what it was. The shop manager told me it was a washing machine for washing clothes and it was new on the market. It was Christmastime. At home, my wife was always washing laundry by hand in the bathtub, which was a tedious job. The washing machine was a perfect gift for my wife for Christmas, so I bought it and told the shopkeeper to deliver it to her on Christmas Day, but he promised to deliver it on Christmas Eve before noon. The machine was delivered in a cardboard box, but nobody wondered what it was. My children thought it was something for me. I came home in the evening and they told me someone had delivered a big box. I pretended I was too tired to look at it, but in the middle of the night I opened the box gently and put a Christmas card on it saying that Santa had brought a washing machine for Mrs. Chand and from now on, she didn't have to wash clothes in the tub. On Christmas Day I assembled the machine properly and washed and dried the clothes by spinning. My wife and children were thrilled to see the machine washing and drying the clothes. The shopkeeper told me I was the first customer to buy the machine from their many stores in 1965.

My wife got a washing machine, and I was desperate to buy a tape recorder. The Grundig tape recorder made in Germany was very popular, but the price was too high for my budget. Every now and then I went into the shop and after looking at the price, I walked away. One day, I asked the shop manager whether there was any chance of the price coming down. He said I would get it at a lower price if I could wait for a month because the Grundig company was going to sell it directly to them, cutting the middleman out. So, I bought a new Grundig recorder for thirty pounds less than the original price, a good deal. We had an old TV, but it still worked and served our purposes.

I worked five days a week, and on Saturday mornings I was in the habit of going to the commercial library near Glasgow Square, in the center of the city. In the basement of the building, there were newspapers and trade magazines. I spent a couple of hours in the library reading papers like the *Manchester Guardian* and the *London Times*. The *Manchester Guardian* was my favorite liberal newspaper. It was well written, and I always looked for news from India. One column writer, Taya Zinkins, had a good grasp of the problems of Indian affairs. These articles were absorbing to me, and I never missed a Zinkins column. Then I used to read the leather industry news. At about twelve thirty, I enjoyed half a glass of beer and a small sandwich in a nearby neat, clean, and quiet pub. Then I went home by bus. Two o'clock was the closing time for pubs, and quite often I used to meet drunk Scotsmen on the road. Sometimes they showered me with abuses and curses, calling me Paki or darkie, which I didn't like at all. For this reason, I never felt completely at home in Glasgow. I'd left India because of caste prejudice and I tried to keep away from bigoted Hindus and Muslims everywhere. I bought a home four miles away from the Gorbals, a predominately Hindu and Muslim area, to save myself from the constant insults and humiliation. The color and caste prejudice and insults hurt me very much.

At two thirty, I usually watched wrestling matches for an hour, and at three thirty I enjoyed watching westerns like *Big Valley* and *Bonanza*. After that, I used to take my wife out shopping until suppertime. This became my routine when I lived in Scotland.

On Sundays, I slept in and then got ready to go see Indian movies. My wife had a habit of making us late for movies, so I used to change the clock so we wouldn't miss the movie or must sit in the front row. Afterward, my wife wanted to go see her friends, so we often visited them on Sunday evenings. In 1966, my wife gave birth to another baby girl. She was a few ounces heavier than my other children, with big eyes, and I called her Raj, but my wife changed her name to Rajrani.

A NEW JOB IN ENGLAND

I was successful in my job at the Clyde Leather Company, and production rose every month. The chairman gave me a small increase in my salary every year for three years. Then the government put a freeze on wages, and the chairman told me that at the end of the year, he couldn't give me a raise because of the government freeze. I was giving him more production, which meant more work and possibly more profit. I wasn't a laborer, and I was rather upset that the chairman wasn't keeping his promise. I reminded him a couple of times that I wasn't under the government freeze as I was technical personnel and in charge of the finishing department of the company, but he didn't budge.

A month passed, and I called the Leather Sellers College to talk to a friend through the secretary of the college. By chance, Dr. Danby, the principal, was there in the office. He asked me how I was getting on at my job. After all, he was the one who got me this job. He said, "If you don't like the job, then go to Leeds. There's a company there looking for an experienced man like you." He gave me the phone number and name of the company and advised me to call them for an appointment.

During the week, I called Leeds and asked for the director of the company. He told me to come by on Saturday morning to meet him. But I had to tell him that on this Saturday I had to work as we were very busy, and my employer would never allow me to take the day off. Then he said to come on Sunday morning, so I booked the sleeper berth on the train and asked the conductor to wake me up and drop me off at Leeds. I took the taxi to meet the director at the factory. He and his secretary were waiting for me with coffee and cookies. It was quite a welcoming atmosphere. I liked English coffee with milk and sugar. The secretary kept pouring more and more coffee and I kept drinking it. We were busy discussing all kinds of subjects over more than an hour. Then I let them know that I had to catch the train back to Glasgow, and I didn't want to miss it, so we should talk about prospective employment. The director said that there was nothing to talk about except salary as Dr. Danby had already told him everything about me. He offered me about 50 percent more money than what I was getting at Clyde and mentioned that the job was in Hull, not in Leeds. Reluctantly I said that I'd thought it was in Leeds. I didn't know much about Hull and would have to talk to my wife. He increased his offer and said, "We don't want you to call your wife." I laughed and agreed that my wife would have no choice. She must go to Hull or stay hungry. I accepted the job offer and he told me he would arrange for me to live in a family home near the factory.

On Monday I went to the Clyde Leather Company office at teatime. The owner and his sons and the secretary were all there. I handed my resignation notice to the owner. There was a momentary hush of dismay throughout the room. Then the boys asked me where I was going to work. I told them in Beverley, England. One boy said he'd worked for that company after graduating from Leeds University. That was it. I told them I would leave in one month and they agreed.

CHAPTER THIRTY

BEVERLEY, YORKSHIRE
1967

Reaching Beverley, Yorkshire, from Glasgow wasn't easy at all since there was no direct train or bus service from Glasgow. I had a mini Morris car, and every Friday I drove to the nearest train station, York, and took the train from York to Edinburgh, then Glasgow. Driving was too difficult on the narrow roads. For about two months, I stayed in a family home in Beverley, and then I bought a house in Hull four miles from the factory and moved my family there. The house in Glasgow was empty, and I locked it and asked my neighbors to check on it every now and then. Hull was a small port city on the Humber and was very quiet. I didn't know anybody there. On the weekends we started going to Wolverhampton as my nephew was living there. Anyhow, I kept myself busy with children and work.

At work, I was given a technical job in the finishing department, but soon I was involved in all sorts of procedures in finishing, color matching, using various dyes and pigments, making samples for customers, and generally supervising machines for leather pressing and other machines. In general, I became a key person in the department. Mr. Warsar was the works manager, a very nice person and a churchman. For four years, I enjoyed working there and gained a lot of experience.

AN OPPORTUNITY IN AMERICA

There was a leather fair in London, and I was sent there with my colleagues. I met an American there who owned a leather manufacturing company in the US. He'd come to the fair to look for new advanced leather machinery. He sat down with a cup of coffee in his hand at the same table where I was sitting alone. He inquired if I was a businessman, and I said no, I was from Beverley representing my company and employed by them in the finishing department. He asked me what sort of work I handled and my responsibilities. He said he was looking for a man like me with a lot of experience and asked me if I would like to go to America. I told him I certainly would if I ever had the chance. He took my address and said he would send the papers once he arrived back home. The talk with the American gave me some encouragement.

Later, I talked to my friend, an old Englishman. He advised me to go to India instead of America. He reminded me that I had enough experience and education to open my own business, which I'd always dreamed of. Plus, he emphasized that there was too much racial prejudice in America, and I would never like it there. I felt discouraged, and I wrote to the American saying that I had changed my mind.

A SWISS FRIEND'S ADVICE

After a few months, my Swiss friend and class fellow from college wrote from America that he was stopping for a few hours at the Glasgow airport and wanted to see me. He was working in America. At the airport, we had lunch together and I happened to tell him I'd rejected an offer to go to America because of the racial prejudice there. He was mad at me. He knew me very well and said I would like it much better there than in the UK. There were a lot of opportunities for me in America and there was no prejudice there. I told him I would take the next opportunity if it ever happened again.

The same week, my wife gave birth to our youngest daughter Savita, a very healthy and lovely baby weighing about two pounds more than our other children.

Few month later, I saw a full-page advertisement in a leather magazine for a leather technologist experienced in all phases of finishing leather. I applied for it. One Saturday morning the postman delivered the mail to my door. My daughter said there were two letters from India, and the third one was a strange-looking letter with a stamp she had never seen. I opened the letter and it was an acceptance letter from the employer in America asking me to apply for a visa. A visa required a marriage and birth certificate, but I had none. I wrote a letter to my parents but got no answer. Time was passing, so Nasib Kaur and I married again in a registry office to get a valid marriage certificate and I succeeded in getting a visa.

Soon I had to tell my colleague Mr. Warsar, the work manager, that I intended to leave the company. He was dismayed. We were very busy, running three shifts, and I was the key person for color matching, sampling, and other responsibilities. He rushed to tell the general manager and sales manager and I was called into the office of the general manager. They asked me why I was leaving, said they couldn't do without me, and offered me a raise. I told them politely that I would never threaten to leave the company where I'd worked diligently for four years for only a few pounds. But I wanted to settle in America, and I had an opportunity to go there.

The general manager said that the company had no hold on me, and I could go anytime with one month's notice, but the problem was that we were very busy running three shifts and it wasn't easy to find a suitable replacement.

I felt very awkward and said hesitantly, "Sir, I wouldn't leave the company in trouble at any cost after making my living here for four years. I'll stay until you find a suitable replacement, whether it takes one month or three." The general manager and the others appreciated my answer very much and thanked me for being very supportive.

A BIG MISTAKE
The news of my plans to go to America went viral and my nephew Harnam Dass, a close friend named Udo Rai, and my younger brother Bhaj Ram suggested that I send my wife and children to live in London in my brother's big house instead of going to my own house in Glasgow. I was reluctant to send my family to my brother's home since I knew he wasn't a very responsible person. I left the decision to my wife, and she wasn't sure where to go. Finally, under a lot of pressure from Udo Rai, Harnam Dass, and others, she decided to go to London. I hired a big truck to carry our belongings to my brother's house two hundred miles away. My wife and children caught the coach to London.

After three weeks, I went to see my family and what I found was disgusting and infuriating. The next day, Udo Rai came, and he apologized for getting my family into this mess. The location of the old house was not good. It was a deserted big house, ready to be demolished. My children were a mess. They were crammed into one big room and looked sickly. They were forced to use newspaper instead of toilet paper in the bathroom. My wife was also in poor health. She'd been working a lot of hours in the shop because my brother refused to charge rent but forced my wife and children to work in the shop and in the house.

Worst of all, my brother's wife had gone to stay with her parents. The whole atmosphere was chaotic. I was very angry with myself and with my wife. I learned through my brother that his wife was arranging a second marriage for her brother, who was already married. I mentioned that bigamy is illegal in the UK. She lashed out at me and shouted that she would pull out every hair of my beard. A relative standing beside me said jokingly that I had no beard. This was a big insult and an interesting way of thanking me for bringing her to the UK from India and helping her bring her parents. She was out of her mind and very insulting. I didn't know what induced her to take this nasty step, what her underlying motives were, or what incentive had lured her to treat me that way. I stayed a day longer, then hired another truck to take my family's belongings to Glasgow four hundred miles away. At the same time, I bought train tickets for my wife and children for Glasgow. When I came back to Hull, I found my driver's license and some other pocket-sized certificates missing. I thought I'd dropped these things somewhere or left them in London. Later, Manu Lal called and told me he saw my driver's license in my brother's pocket. I tried to forget that my brother and his family had ever existed before I left for America.

My brother moved to Wolverhampton when his house in London was demolished. I visited my nephew Harnam Dass, and some friends forced me to go to my brother's house to attend a birthday party for his son. I stayed there for a few minutes and then walked out, and I never returned to Wolverhampton. Harnam Dass kept telling me about my brother and his wife, saying that they weren't getting along well, but I didn't want to listen and frankly had no interest. After all, they were husband and wife and grown up. I was a foreigner to them, and I had suffered enough. I had more than enough of my own problems because my family was divided across different countries, and I was in a fix.

After about a year, I visited Glasgow and learned from my nephew that my brother's wife had disappeared, and no one had seen her for twelve days. This bad news sent a shockwave throughout the family. I had a few days' leave and wanted to spend time with my family, but my wife insisted that we go to Wolverhampton and check on their children, thinking more about our moral duty.

After two months, around Christmastime, the general manager at my company in Leeds told me that they had found a replacement and I could arrange to go to America. On December 19 or 20, Mr. Warsar met me in the morning and thanked me for my service to the company. At the same time, he asked if I would be going to Glasgow to spend a few days with my family, and I said yes. Then he asked if I would come back after Christmas and then return to spend the New Year with them, and I said yes. He said he had a better proposition and he would see me in a couple of hours. He came back just after the morning teatime and told me I could leave that day for Glasgow and have a ten- to twelve-day paid holiday from the company to enjoy my stay with my family before going to America. He would make sure my salary and other benefits were paid in time. Before I said goodbye to everybody, they loaded me up with bottles of scotch whiskeys and wine, cash, and so many other gifts I could hardly carry it all. In the meantime, I told my wife in Glasgow that I would be with her that evening. She was surprised and happy and asked me to bring some leather for the children's school bags. Mr. Warsar brought a small bundle of leather and put it in my car. I said goodbye to him and left Beverley for good at the end of 1969.

A HARD DECISION

I didn't know then whether it was a good or bad move to go to America and leave my wife and children in Glasgow. Surely, I didn't like to part with my family, but it was my habit enforced by my responsibilities to look ahead and try to solve my troubles. I was very conscious of my successes and failures and always assessed what I'd gained or lost. Scotland had been good to me in many ways. I had a house, I had an old car, I had children, and they were getting educated as planned. I had my own education and a good job, but I had no savings. Why? I knew the answer, but I was helpless. I wasn't a spendthrift, and my wife wasn't wasteful; it was all due to bad company. I'd never had a good Indian friendship or good Indian company in the UK, except for Shiv Raj who was in India. People ran to me when they needed help because most of them were illiterate or thought I had a lot of money. They were selfish backstabbers. I was arranging marriages for other people's children, helping to bring them to the UK, and paying for other people's funerals and weddings. People were taking advantage of me, and I knew it, but I was helpless because this habit of helping others was embedded in me from a young age. My good father often told me that what is the use of education and living if we can't help the needy ones. I felt happy when I helped others, but now it was hurting me, too. After so many years of hard work, I had no bank balance. I knew people wouldn't stop coming to me and I wouldn't stop helping them. Some people cried in front of me if I did not agree with them. I was weak and it was a mistake.

Another burning issue was caste prejudice. I left India because of this horrible cancer, but I found the same problem in the UK as more and more Hindus and Muslims immigrated there from India and Pakistan. The problem of prejudice was getting worse, but there were other factors that compelled me to leave in search of a happier and more successful life. I was forty years old, and I wasn't satisfied with my life. The best years of my life, if not gone, were slipping away; the only way to solve all my problems was to leave the country and the rotten people full of caste cancer behind. My brother and other relatives were selfish and had no love for me or my family. They had proved a serious liability for me. Moving to the US for a job was a good excuse to leave all these problems behind and try my luck elsewhere. But it was a bold and dangerous decision to uproot my family once again in search of full freedom and peace.

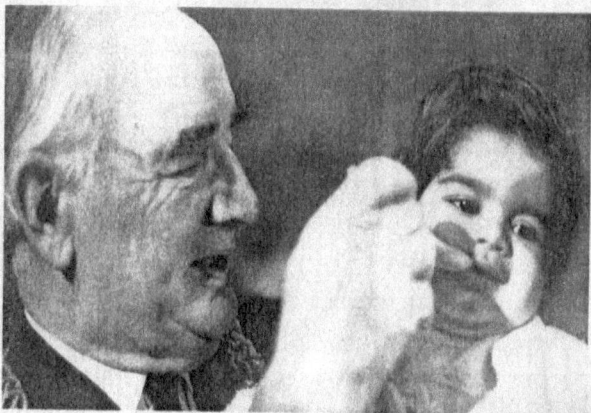

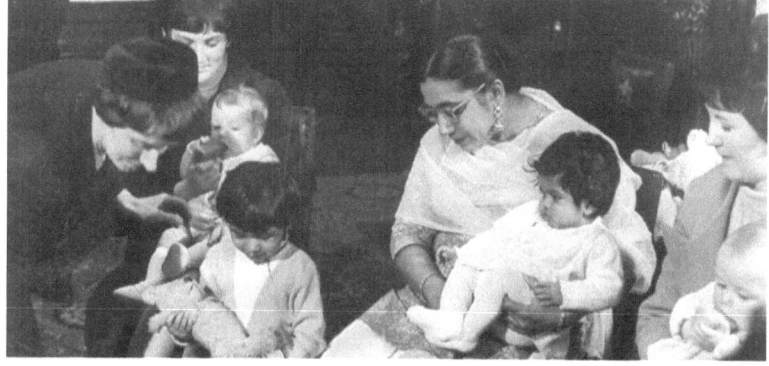

Top: My children and I (1970)
Middle: My daughter Savita with Lord Provost (1969)
Bottom: My wife and children in Glasgow City Chambers (1969)

CHAPTER THIRTY ONE

THE UNITED STATES
1970

I received my airline ticket from the company in America. I was booked to fly to Boston, Massachusetts, on January 8, 1970. This was my first visit to America, and I was a little apprehensive. It was a difficult decision, and just the thought of it scared me. However, the journey was long, and I flew from Glasgow to London, then from London to Boston. The flight was delayed by about two hours and I reached Boston just before midnight. As soon as I deplaned, someone met me and took me to immigration. I handed over my immigration papers and the gentleman introduced me to the superintendent of the company. I collected my baggage and we drove fifty miles to a small place called Hamber.

On the road we stopped at a restaurant to eat. Everything was new to me and I enjoyed the food, especially the fresh salad and tomatoes. The road looked very strange, completely different from Scotland, full of big, bright signs and blinding lights. Finally, he dropped me off at a hotel near the firm. Early the next morning, the owner of the company, Mr. Home, showed up. He introduced himself to me, took me to the factory, and quietly handed me a few hundred dollars to spend before I got my first paycheck. I was quite happy because I needed the money.

The factory building was quite new and resembled a big open hall under one roof. Mr. Home gave me a tour of the factory and introduced me to the staff. The firm was importing half-tanned goatskins from India and Pakistan and after manufacturing, it sold them to ladies' shoe manufacturers and glove manufacturers. This was the first time I had a chance to deal with goatskins. In England, I'd had experience with splits and side leather. The environment of this company was totally different from the one in England. A lot of employees were immigrants from neighboring poor countries, unable to speak proper English. The first few days passed, and I met the staff and some workers. Then the superintendent and the owner met with me and decided to give me a chance to develop new leathers. I had some experience, but this was completely new. In England, I was well respected by the staff and workers and they looked to me for instructions. Here, the workers were scared and jealous, and they didn't want any foreigners around except their own countrymen. Even the veteran workers thought I was going to replace them. They did their best to make sure that I didn't succeed. It was hard for me to complain about older employees who had been there for a long time and were faithful to the company.

I tried different things on a small scale but was unable to reproduce them on a large scale. I was losing heart. The employer raised my salary, asked me to supervise the tanning, and tried to set up a lab for me, but I was fed up with the separation from my wife and children and it was hard to reach them. I didn't have a phone in Glasgow, and I didn't want to disturb the neighbor, Mrs. McDevitt, although she enjoyed receiving calls from me. After three months, the employer paid my fare and sent me to visit my family in Glasgow. The town of Hamber was small and very quiet, and I hadn't found any Indian people for company.

At the nearby YMCA, I met a young fellow from South India who seemed to be in poor condition. I didn't go into his personal affairs but asked him if he wanted some good clothes as he was dressed in very poor-quality, light clothing for winter. I gave him my best, and my old Harris Tweed woolen jacket and trousers fit him nicely. He told me about Indian movies that some Indian students were showing at Boston University on the weekends, but I didn't have a car, so I started traveling fifty miles to Boston by bus to see Indian movies. One time, I missed the bus and had to spend the night at the bus station.

MY FIRST VISIT TO NEW YORK

One long weekend I traveled to New York, two hundred miles away, on a Greyhound bus and stayed at the YMCA because I didn't have much money. Any money I was paid, I was sending to Glasgow, so my wife had enough to spend. It was crazy to see what was then the world's tallest building, the Empire State Building. I also saw the United Nations headquarters and other landmarks. At night, I visited Forty-Second Street, which is famous for movies theaters, bright lights, and lot of traffic. Soon I was elbowed by a strong girl and I fell into the middle of the street. Some passersby helped me up and a policeman appeared on the scene. I wasn't hurt, but the policeman wanted to know what happened. I told him I was new to New York and had come to see a movie, and that I was staying at the YMCA. He advised me to go back to the YMCA, keep away from alleys and big buildings, and walk near the edge of the pavement. If I wanted to go out, I should go with friends. This was my first experience visiting New York.

I tried to go to Glasgow to see my family now and then on a long weekend, but it cost me too much although my employer didn't mind giving me a day off. Then an older person at the company who happened to be a partner in the firm became very friendly with me. He showed up every Sunday or Saturday at my apartment and took me out for the day in his Cadillac. We traveled a lot throughout New Hampshire and Vermont and nearly reached the border of Canada. He wasn't lacking in money, so he fed me well on these tours. I was feeling very lonely and sick and I realized I had made a mistake by coming to America. I had no phone in my apartment, so I called my family from pay phones, but it was too expensive even for a short call. I did everything I could to reach my family without concern for the money.

One Sunday afternoon, my company friend took me to a very nice beach in New Hampshire. The day was sunny and warm. He decided to go into the water and coaxed me to go with him. I had no experience swimming in the ocean. He met some lady friends swimming there and joined them. In no time, I found myself in deep water. The waves pulled me in deeper and I was afraid I would drown. Luckily, I had flippers on, and I had learned a little bit of swimming at the YMCA. So, by asking God's help and with the help of the flippers, I made it out of the water but decided not to go into the ocean again.

One day, the office gave me a letter my wife had forwarded from my father to the factory address. In it, my father admonished me sternly to send my wife to India as her mother was very sick and she wanted to see her daughter. He said he couldn't endure the thought of her mother dying without seeing her. Plus, my father said that he'd never asked me for anything before and this was his request, to send my wife to India to see her mother. I felt sorry and emotional; after all, she was my good mother-in-law. The owner asked me if everything was all right and I told him the truth. He was aware of my circumstances and that I was homesick. He said if I wanted to go, it would be all right with him.

MY FIRST VISIT TO NIAGARA FALLS

There was a Labor Day holiday and I decided to go to Canada to see Niagara Falls before I went back to Glasgow. I took the Greyhound bus in the evening and after traveling all night, I reached Niagara Falls in the early morning. I spent all day there, enjoying the falls. I went on a boat and bought a plastic poncho to go near the falls. It was a wonderful experience.

In the evening, I decided to go to a hotel for the night. There were several big and small hotels, but I found a notice of "no vacancy" everywhere and I didn't know what that meant. At the reception desk, they told me the hotel was full. Finally, I asked the gentleman behind the counter the meaning of *no vacancy*. He told me it meant the hotel was full. I grew worried as I was tired from running around on foot looking for a room. Then I explained that this was my first time at Niagara Falls, and I hadn't expected it to be so crowded. He joked that the easiest way to spend the night was to go to the police station. I think he meant jail. I started blushing. Then he suggested I try my luck at private homes. I went to about ten houses and the answer was negative every time. Finally, an old lady said no, but after a couple of seconds, she said she was expecting somebody, but she didn't think he was coming. She said that she had a big room and it would cost me forty dollars to rent it for the night. I didn't ask her any further questions, just took my wallet out and gave her the money. I locked the door, laid on the bed with my clothes on, and fell asleep. When I awoke, it was early morning. I was feeling good and as soon as the sun was up, I left the room and went straight to the Greyhound bus station and booked my seat to Boston. Then I visited the beautiful gardens and walked around before catching the bus to Boston in the evening.

Mr. Home advised me to go to India and open my own business there and he would market anything I made in America, whether it was goatskins or any other leather. He promised to give me all his old machinery. This was very nice of him and gave me a lot of encouragement before I left for Glasgow after a month's notice near the end of 1970.

Visiting Washington D.C. with my wife and daughter Rajrani (1977)

CHAPTER THIRTY TWO

MY WIFE'S VISIT TO INDIA
1971

After my return from America in December 1970, Nasib Kaur refused to go to India. She was worried about our young children. I told her that I would stay and look after them. Finally, I put her on a plane after sixteen years in Scotland. My nephew received her at the Delhi airport and accompanied her home. She visited her mother the next day. Her mother was very sick and unable to speak, but her eyes communicated her happiness at seeing her daughter. After a few days, she passed away.

My wife was in the prime of her health when she left for India. My mother loved having her company in the house. My mother wanted to visit all her old relatives and my wife was also very fond of seeing them. So, they traveled on foot and by tonga everywhere. Eventually, Nasib Kaur decided to stay longer in the company of my mother. I phoned her and wrote to her but received no response. My mother told me to come back with the children. She would book the seats. I was frustrated as Nasib Kaur had been gone for a month. Three months passed and I was out of a job. I was running out of money and I wasn't qualified to get unemployment.

Finally, she came back after four months and she was a changed woman. I was surprised at her declarations that my father was wiser than me. He had a lot of guts, and that was why he was rich, she said. I had no guts and I would never become rich. She started comparing me with my father. In a sense she was right, but she was also wrong. My father was a businessman and I was a worker. My focus was on educating my children and bettering ourselves and I was in the red till my youngest daughter, Savita, finished her college education. My father and I simply had different priorities. Nasib Kaur was a simple village person and all she knew was her simple daily chores. She was overwhelmed by my father's success and his business dealings, but she did not understand the importance and depth of the things I was doing. My whole life was made by big challenges and guts, and when she found out I had saving accounts under her name in both India and the UK, and later that I had bought land and sold it for great profits, she apologized and laughed, saying that she had not meant anything by what she said.

BACK TO AMERICA

However, I was out of a job, and one day I visited my old firm in Neilston on my way to the seaside. I learned that the owner had passed away. His sons offered me my old job and I took it, but things weren't the same. In the meantime, my eldest daughter, Kamlesh, finished high school and took a job as a shorthand typist in a nearby office. My other daughter, Shukesh, was not doing well in school. It wasn't her fault, but in my absence, the school system had changed a lot. I was very disheartened because I was failing and not giving my children the education, they needed. So, I applied for their visas to take them to America. My wife wasn't happy to go to America and she was listening too much to our Scottish neighbors, who said she wouldn't be happy there. The truth was that after spending about a year in America, I no longer liked Scotland. I felt free in America, but in Glasgow, my friends were again after me to arrange matches for their children. As usual, I was unable to refuse them. I felt more caste prejudice as more Muslims and Hindus were pouring into Glasgow. I wanted to get away from these people and away from my brothers and nephews.

I knew a lot of chemical sales agents in America and one day I called one of them to see if there were any companies looking for a leather technologist. He promised to call me back in a few days. Instead, I got a call from an employer in Boston who wanted me to go there and start working with them. This time, I took my two daughters with me and we landed in Boston in one foot of snow. We had prearranged for an apartment in the small town of Salem. The next day, I went to work and told my daughters to sleep well as they were tired. My eldest daughter Kamlesh went downstairs for milk and bought a local newspaper. There were so many openings for shorthand typists. After having a cup of tea, she asked the shopkeepers how to get to Boston and she went and got a job.

She worked for eight hours and came home before I got back. I was surprised when she told me that she'd already found a job and gone to work there that morning after I left. After a few months with this company, she found a better job at the Massachusetts Institute of Technology (MIT) in Cambridge. There she met an older man from Pakistan who happened to be doing research there. He thought my daughter was from Pakistan as she was dressed in Punjabi clothes.

My daughter, without a second thought, invited him to visit me for company's sake. He was a jolly good fellow from Karachi Jinnah University, a professor. We enjoyed his company on the weekends.

My other daughter, Shukesh, stayed at home. We had no car, so we walked for shopping and we were unable to go very far. I worried a lot about her becoming bored or homesick, so I always tried to cheer her up. We were eating bread most of the time as Kamlesh was working and it was too much for her to make chapati after working hours. She needed rest, too, after traveling to and from Boston. We were living in Salem in an old apartment. Shukesh understood that her father and sister were busy, and she wasn't working at home. She showed initiative without any pressure from her sister and me. After all, she had grown up in the company of her mother, who was a perfect chapati maker. Shukesh made balls out of atta, then threw them in the air and tried to catch them. Sometimes they fell on the ground.

I didn't get angry at her but told her to be happy and do what she wanted. Finally, after some hits and misses, plus a little help from her sister, she succeeded in making chapati and we liked her homemade chapati better than bread. I did my best to keep both daughters happy in case they got homesick. Now we had a phone for the first time, and I let them talk to their mother and sisters in Glasgow. Then I took Shukesh to school. They reviewed her education and the teacher decided she should learn accounting as a major in high school. She loved her program and graduated from high school, then found a part-time job working on the weekends for pocket money.

MY OLD CAR CHARLIE

There were two policemen in my neighborhood who wanted to sell their old cars to me for $1,300, but I didn't want them because I thought they were too expensive. Then one day, while I was at the grocery store, one policeman hunted me down and told me he wanted to sell the car. I asked how much, and he said $350. He told me he was buying a Cadillac he liked, and he was short that amount. So, I gave in because it was a bargain. I took him to my bank right away and gave him the money in cash. He put the car under my name and registered it. The car was a Pontiac and we named it Charlie. From then on, we were able to see movies in Boston and travel here and there over long distances.

MY DAUGHTER'S MARRIAGE

One day I received a letter from my brother-in-law, Mr. Shiv Raj, in New Delhi about a young man who had finished his master's degree in engineering in America. Shiv Raj knew his family and he advised me to meet the young man as a perfect candidate to marry my daughter Kamlesh. I wrote a letter of introduction to the boy, Siri Ram. He was anxious and came to stay with us for a couple of days in Salem. He met my children and liked my daughter, and she had no objection. After finding that they liked each other, I tried to talk to my wife in Glasgow and get her to come to America so we could arrange the marriage there. We were all busy working and it was easy for her to come to America, but she was angry with me for deciding about the marriage without consulting her and she didn't want to come. It took some time, but I listened to her. She was, after all, Kamlesh's mother. She had gone through a lot of hard work to raise her daughter, and finally she said that the wedding must be performed in Glasgow, where we had lived for the last twenty-two years and where her friends were. We had to agree with her.

My daughters and I took a leave from work for a week and flew to Glasgow. We knew a family from Pakistan, and they extended their help. Mrs. McDevitt, our neighbor, also helped us plan the wedding. Siri Ram flew to Birmingham, to his relatives' home, and traveled to Glasgow with the marriage party, about three hundred miles. It wasn't easy for anybody to make that round trip in a single day after attending a wedding. I was, without a lot of time and help, coming all the way from America, and arranging a quick marriage, hotel accommodations, etc., wasn't easy. but a Pakistani friend suggested that the marriage party use his empty house, which was very nice of him and I greatly appreciated it. He also gathered chairs from his and his brothers' homes and brought them to me when he learned that the local gurdwara couldn't loan them to me because I'd forgotten to invite the man in charge of the gurdwara furniture. My friends, nephews, and cousins all came from England and the wedding was performed in the local gurdwara according to Indian tradition in 1975. Afterward, we went back to Salem, Massachusetts.

Top: My wife (1971)
Bottom: My house in Jallandhar Cantt. in India

CHAPTER THIRTY THREE

BIG CHANGES AND CHOICES

I had my two daughters Kamlesh and Shukesh to keep me company, but I still missed my other children and my wife. My wife was also lonely without our eldest daughters, who were grown and often helped her. We didn't like the Boston area very much because of the severely cold winters. I saw an advertisement in a leather magazine and applied for a position in Philadelphia. The general manager of the company accepted my application and asked me to come to Philadelphia for an interview. He met me at the airport, and we had lunch together. He discussed the job and salary and agreed to hire me for the position. Then, we drove to the factory and he gave me a confirmation letter and a check for my plane fare. I toured the factory before he put me on the plane to Boston.

VISITING PHILADELPHIA

Philadelphia was new to me, and I'd never driven over long distances or to big cities. But there was no other way, so I took my old car to the repair shop and asked them to check it thoroughly and change the oil. I left Salem in the early morning before rush hour and drove carefully on the highway, stopping every fifty or sixty miles in case the engine heated up. I reached Philadelphia in the afternoon and the general manager put me up in a hotel called Hilton, in the middle of the city, a couple of miles from the factory. I'd never lived in the middle of a city with heavy traffic and I wasn't keen on staying there. In the morning, the general manager and other company leaders asked me about my stay in the hotel, so I replied that I wasn't used to living in big cities. They found a place for me in New Jersey on Route 38. It was beautiful, with all glass doors in the bedroom, kitchen, and bathroom, and I lived there for six weeks before I found an apartment in Haddon Heights near White Horse Pike in New Jersey.

OUR MOVE TO NEW JERSEY

My daughters came from Salem to New Jersey, and while we were living in Haddon Heights, we started looking for a house to buy. The location was important as my children had to go to school and colleges and the family had to go shopping. We bought a big house in Collingswood in New Jersey, just off White Horse Pike, only five miles from my job, and half a mile from the schools in Collingswood.

After buying the house, I needed furniture and beds before I would bring my children and wife from Glasgow. I went to a big store and bought one bed. It was expensive, as I knew my wife's taste wasn't cheap. I was short on money, so I gave the store whatever I had and told them I would pay the rest in a week and then take the bed home. The salesperson tried to talk to me about a credit card, but I refused to listen to him and walked away with the receipt. After a week, I went back with the rest of the money, paid the full price, and picked up the bed. This time, the salesperson brought his manager to talk to me. He was a nice person, but without listening to him, I kept telling him that I didn't want this furniture on pay up. When I had cash, I'd buy it. I never bought stuff on pay up and didn't know about credit cards. Finally, he said simply that I could have furniture without paying anything. He explained to me that I should take advantage of the credit card scheme and pay the bills on time. I got a credit card for the first time and bought furniture for the whole house.

After a couple of weeks, my wife and children came from Glasgow and landed at Kennedy Airport in New York. Then we drove to New Jersey.

The general manager of the factory I'd begun working at was also a leather tanner and the firm was owned by a company in New York. He asked me to supervise the tanning department. Then, after a month, he told me that the second shift was a mess and he had no reliable person to supervise it, so he put me in charge of all second shift operations. The workers were mainly Mexicans and African Americans. I was the only person of Indian origin in the firm. The workers resisted my authority wholeheartedly. They had plans to go to a nearby pub one by one. A couple of employees were cheating on the time clock. They told some other junior employees to clock them out at later hours after they had left much earlier. Some of the young employees were using the company phone to talk to their friends while leaving the machines running unattended. It took me a couple of weeks to find the main mischief mongers, but once someone was sacked, the others started obeying and respecting me.

Then there were a lot of problems in the leather industry. I learned when I was in England about the development of a synthetic material that looked exactly like leather, called Corfam. It was a lot cheaper than real leather and we knew that sooner or later this synthetic material would be used for shoe uppers. Another problem was that third world countries like India and Pakistan had learned the manufacturing techniques and were exporting finished leather instead of raw material. A lot of companies specializing in fine leather were closing because raw materials like goatskins were no longer readily available to them, and others were closing because they couldn't compete with imports. We were losing customers, too, and the company replaced the general manager with another general manager. He was also unable to fix the problems, and finally the company decided to close the plant and slowly started laying off workers. I was the last one to leave the firm. I had worked there for several years and was approaching retiring age.

At home, our children were in high school and two were attending Rutgers University. It was becoming very hard to find a suitable job, and there were more experienced men out of a job than there were available jobs. The future of the leather-making industry in the US was very dim. Some leather manufacturers moved overseas to make leather because of the cheap labor and availability of raw material.

OUR MOVE TO MILWAUKEE: 1982

Finally, someone from Milwaukee, Wisconsin, responded to the ad I'd posted for a job and asked me to come to Milwaukee for an interview. The company was making split leathers, as I had in Scotland, and I was hired to run the second shift. There was no other way except to go to Milwaukee, and that required me to uproot my family yet again if I wanted to stay in the leather-making industry. So, I moved my family to Milwaukee, but that proved to be a mistake as after three years I was out of a job again. I was aware that sooner or later, all the factories would be closed in Milwaukee, the center of the leather industry in America.

I was worried, and I started going to MATC to learn domestic appliance repairs as a backup career. I got a diploma in 1985 after attending classes for one year. This gave me some satisfaction that I could still work if I couldn't find a job in the leather manufacturing industry. By then we had three daughters at Wisconsin University in Milwaukee, and they were staying at home. I had a lot of expenses and I didn't want to stop my daughters from going to university. I decided to sell my house in New Jersey. I managed to sell the house quite easily with a little bit of profit, but that money lasted less than six months. I was making a small amount of money by repairing appliances, but it was a strenuous job and I got hurt slightly a couple of times. My wife and children got scared and asked me to stop doing the repair work.

Luckily, my daughter Raksha Devi was working on a master's degree and went to St. Francis hospital once a week. She saw a post on the notice board for a part time job and suggested I apply for it. I was adamant about only working in the leather manufacturing industry, but I was aware I stood no chance. Finally, I decided to go see where the hospital was and what kind of job it was. I got the job, working on weekends as a security officer. The first thing that attracted me was that the job was neat and clean and required a lot of walking, and I was looking for exercise. As I was usually working the night shift, I started going to MATC again during the daytime, and I earned a diploma in heating and air conditioning in 1989. I happened to like the job in the hospital as a security officer as I was among educated nurses and doctors all the time and I became friendly or acquainted with them. Soon the hospital offered me full-time work, and I agreed. Some doctors advised me to attend small courses as this was the only way to get ahead in the job and earn more money. I progressed very well and later the hospital gave me permission to work as much as I wanted. At first, I planned to work for only six months or so at the hospital, but time passed, and I worked there for eleven years.

My wife was visiting our house in Scotland when she got sick and I had to take an emergency leave and stay there for a few months. The hospital asked me to either come back or resign from the job. So, I decided to resign at the age of seventy, in 2001, as my wife's health wasn't good, and she needed my attention. Otherwise, this job would have been good enough until retirement.

Top: Visiting our good friends Mary and Paul McBride in Glasgow, Scotland (1976)
Middle Left: Savita's High School Graduation (1986)
Middle Right: Rajrani's College Graduation (1990)
Bottom: Family group photo

UNIVERSITY OF WISCONSIN - MILWAUKEE

THE BOARD OF REGENTS OF THE UNIVERSITY OF WISCONSIN SYSTEM
ON THE NOMINATION OF THE FACULTY OF
COLLEGE OF LETTERS AND SCIENCE

HAS CONFERRED UPON

KAMALA CHAND

THE DEGREE OF

BACHELOR OF ARTS

TOGETHER WITH ALL HONORS, RIGHTS, AND PRIVILEGES BELONGING TO
THAT DEGREE. IN WITNESS WHEREOF, THIS DIPLOMA IS GRANTED.
GIVEN AT MILWAUKEE IN THE STATE OF WISCONSIN, THIS FOURTEENTH DAY OF MAY,
NINETEEN HUNDRED EIGHTY-NINE.

Shukesh And Raksha's College Graduation from Rutgers University (1980)

CHAPTER THIRTY FOUR

NASIB KAUR'S RETURN TO INDIA
1977

After nourishing all her hopes and dreams into reality, Nasib Kaur felt free and confident and asked me if she could take a trip to India. She wanted to see her relatives and friends there. She had made a solemn promise to my parents to build a small house on the family property in the village according to their wishes, but unfortunately, they passed away in 1974, before she arrived in 1977. Also, she encountered a lot of opposition from my brothers since my parents were no longer there. We'd never anticipated this; it was a wake-up call, but it was unacceptable.

Opportunists began to cause trouble, and the house-building scheme became an enviable situation. But she didn't give up and kept her promise with great solemnity after I told her we owned one-fourth of everything my father had left behind. My good father had owned thirty to thirty-five acres of land. Over the next five years, she visited India many times with determination and managed to build a small house with a big boundary surrounding it. My brothers did everything possible to stop her. A lot of chilling prospects emerged, and it seemed we were constantly wrestling with a huge life crisis or difficult challenges. We found ourselves surrounded by vultures who wanted to prey on us. They broke into the house and stole expensive articles; they cut our beautiful ornamental trees and bushes and did all kinds of damage. None of these horrible events depressed or deterred her but made her more adamant to stick to the solemn promise she'd made to my parents.

Finally, they made an organized and determined effort to stop her from collecting disability benefits in Scotland. Such malice is unparalleled in the history of the world, and by repeated false complaints, my brothers Bhaj Ram and Bhagu Ram succeeded in stopping her from getting benefits for a period of two years. She had a house in Glasgow and lived there for a long time. Because her family lived in America, it was nearly impossible to sort out her problems. But she was free to travel back and forth to Glasgow. I advised her to give up her struggle, and her dear, trusted friends in Glasgow Mary and her mother Mrs. McDevitt told her to forget about the disability claims, but she was in pain, and she was angry. It wasn't a question of losing money, but she felt deeply she was accused of making false claims because she suffered from chronic arthritis. She persisted in making inquiries and finally flew to Glasgow to visit a government agency that could help her. The agency filed a case against the government disability department for unlawfully stopping the benefits. They won the case in my wife's favor and she was awarded far more benefits and back pay than what she'd expected because she didn't claim all the entitlements. This decision made my brothers extremely angry as they'd failed to stop a woman they had always viewed as inferior to them from getting benefits.

AN ONWARD JOURNEY

Finally, they took forcible possession of her house in Nai-Abadi, Nakodar. She'd built it with extreme hard labor and great passion to spend time with the family and the village community she loved and fulfill her sacred promise to my parents. As an outsider, she found it very hard to deal with the corrupt police and counterfeit lawyers to get our house back. She was among wrong people and she was worried about her own safety, plus it was a time -consuming process to go to courts where judges and juries were for sale and she was not willing to buy. She shouted for my help, but I was too busy with my job and making up for our losses. By calculating everything that place is not worth for our living there, I advised Nasib Kaur to come back to the United States and let them do what they want. We wanted a peaceful life for our children and for us and decided to lose our house and forget everything. This decision pained her too much.

TRUSTING THE WRONG PEOPLE

She was victimized and deceived by unscrupulous, sinister, and greedy my brothers and some relatives she had thought throughout her life were her own dear ones. Acute pain was written on her face. This was a big blow to her, and she never recovered from the shock. Since she was a woman, my three brothers couldn't tolerate her deep sense of wisdom, dexterity, and self-esteem.

She always thought of how we could improve ourselves and help others. She did her best to help poor relatives, neighbors, and others so they could have a better life, but none of them appreciated her efforts. Instead, they betrayed her and became enemies and that was our very bad luck.

My wife never got better, and over time, she developed cancer and passed away at the age of seventy-five while visiting her house in Glasgow with me. Her children and grandchildren, her friends, all came to Scotland from America and England to say farewell to their beloved one. She left a wonderful legacy and sweet memories to her family, friends, and neighbors. Her hard work and timeless wisdom made all the difference to her daughters and her husband. We all miss her very much and pray for her soul to rest in peace. She loved the Scottish hills and scenery and clean water streams. Her remains after cremation were scattered in a quiet corner of a beautiful lake among the lovely green hills outside Glasgow as this was a part of the country she loved most and visited with me many times in the summer months. We pay homage to this wonderful lady whenever we go to Glasgow, Scotland.

My house in Nai-abadi, Nakodar, India

CHAPTER THIRTY FIVE

DEDICATIONS AND DISAPPOINTMENTS

My distant cousin Shenker Rai, who had accompanied me from India, worked in Inverness, Scotland, for two years. He paid all the money back to the uncle who had loaned it. Then he gave up his job and came back to Glasgow. His wife and two sons were still living back home in India. He wanted to open a grocery shop, but he had no collateral. Finally, he convinced me with the help of his friends to provide collateral since I owned a house, and thus opened the grocery store. I wanted him to succeed, so I rented the small shop of his choice in my name. He was supposed to work hard to run the store but got mixed up with bad company and started drinking and partying. He kept the shop for six months, but failed to pay the rent, and thus had to close the store in 1957. The owner demanded the rent, and I ended up paying eighty pounds out of my own pocket since my name was on the lease. The owner threatened to take me to court if I didn't pay.

Shenker Rai was expected to send money to his wife, but he was out of work. Meanwhile, she was wreaking havoc within the family in India. Finally, my father asked me to arrange for his wife to come to

Scotland, but my cousin didn't want her there since he'd taken up with a mistress in Glasgow. My father was financially supporting Shenker Rai's family. Under pressure from my father and my distant uncle (Shenker Rai's father), I sponsored his wife to come to Scotland 1959. She came, but she was also very irresponsible. I begged my friends in Birmingham to find a job for him. They helped and he worked there for six months, but then passed away due to spinal issues in 1965. It was summer and I was getting ready for a vacation with my family when I received the telegram about his death. Instead I traveled to Birmingham to arrange and pay for his funeral and bring his wife to Glasgow because the relatives in Birmingham didn't want to take any responsibility for an uneducated woman and her daughter.

In Glasgow, I did everything to keep her happy, but she was nothing but trouble and was in bad health. Then she and her friends pressured me to apply for her two sons living in India to come to Scotland, and I had to sponsor them. Finally, the children arrived, and they began attending school and adjusting to the environment. The older boy found a job as a bus driver with the Glasgow Corporation. The younger one was a cook in a restaurant. Both got married, but both died young; one committed suicide, and the other died of a heart attack. I did my best to help them and to please my distant uncle and my father, but they did the wrong things and met the wrong people. My hopes to make them better were dashed.

In July 1961, Bhaj Ram, my younger brother, came to the UK as a student. He flew to London, then took the train, but he didn't have enough money left for the full train fare to Glasgow. He neglected to inform me that he was flying to London on a certain date. In London at Euston Railway Station, he bought a train ticket with whatever money he had to Wigan Station, only halfway to Glasgow. I was at work and had no clue that he was coming to the UK, that he was in London, or that he was out of money.

With the very small amount of money he had left, he sent a telegram from Wigan that he was in Wigan and had no money to come to Glasgow. Luckily, my wife was at home when the telegram came. She immediately went next door and asked Mrs. McDevitt to go to Glasgow Railway Station with her, and she paid for his ticket to Glasgow. He arrived on the next train. It wasn't a very smart move on his part not to ensure he had enough money to finish the trip.

I came home a little late from work and he opened the door and hugged me and lifted me as a gesture of brotherly love. After a couple of months, I sent him to Wolverhampton, England, for the holidays so he could meet his Indian friends there. He stayed with a family who had no education and no notion to educate their children, and a long time passed before he returned to Glasgow. I noted a change in his attitude and saw that he wasn't very enthusiastic about his studies. He was very skeptical. I felt rather brokenhearted. Although some other people warned me to find work for him and not to spend money on his education, I didn't want to listen to anyone. I was determined to send him to college in Northampton. I didn't want to play around with his college education, and I didn't know the repercussions of not sending him to college when I arranged for him to come and study.

So, I arranged for his lodging with my old Polish

landlady, Mrs. Noga, and put him on the train to Northampton. I had already paid his tuition. My wife took the responsibility of paying for his lodging. Every month, she bought a postal order from the Dennistoun post office and sent it to Mrs. Noga. We were a little tight on money, but I never bothered to tell my wife. I took a loan of £300 from an old couple living on the Isle of Arran (outside of Glasgow) and put my house up as collateral. In 1963, Bhaj Ram completed his two-year studies.

He never bothered to tell me whether he passed his final exams, but I guessed he didn't. A big consolation was that he got a job as a chargehand, or foreman, in a boot and shoe factory in London not far from our place of residence. He was married, and his wife Viya was in India staying with my parents. Since Bhaj Ram's studies were ending, I wrote to my folks a couple of times to apply for Viya's passport, but they didn't bother responding. I traveled to India to apply for her passport, and later my father booked her passage. She arrived in London about a month before I finished my studies in June 1964. Since my brother and I were staying in one room and had no extra accommodations, we decided to send Viya to Glasgow, where my family was living and had plenty of room. As soon as I was finished with college, I flew back home to Glasgow, and on the same day, I put Viya on a plane to London to her husband and they began living together.

I think Viya found a job and started working. After a year or so, she forced her husband to quit his shoe factory job and they opened a small general store in the middle of London in an old building that was fit to be demolished. She was very anxious to bring her parents and siblings from India. She demanded my help, and I sent her my house's title deed. She didn't respond to say whether she'd received the documents. After a month, I phoned her to ask about it. She answered very abruptly and in inappropriate language, which wasn't very nice of her. I was very disappointed. I didn't tell my brother or my wife about her insulting behavior and remarks. I tried to console myself by reasoning that she was a city girl and city people aren't respectful to their elders like village folks.

However, she succeeded in bringing her parents and siblings from India to England in 1968. The entire family was illiterate, and they became a burden and liability to Bhaj Ram. In the meantime, her father started heavy drinking, thinking big, proud and did the wrong things. My brother didn't like this, and trouble started brewing between my brother, his father-in-law, and his wife Viya. I heard about this through other people, but I stayed out of it as I'd had enough of them. They proved selfish.

Sometime in 1971, their house was demolished, the whole family moved to Wolverhampton from London, and more and more arguments started between my brother and his wife. She wanted to help her parents and her siblings, but he had some limitations and was reluctant to spend too much money on his in-laws. Fights and arguments became quite common in the house, even in front of their young children. They were unhappy. Finally, in 1973, she disappeared, leaving behind her baby daughter, only a few weeks old, and their three other children under six years of age. No one had seen her going anywhere or heard any noise as she disappeared in the nighttime. I was living in America and learned of her disappearance twelve days later, when I visited my family in Glasgow.

My wife and I visited Wolverhampton and saw their young children in very poor condition, and we took two of them to Glasgow. Later, we were accused of kidnapping. Everything I did for my brother and his wife was a waste of time and money and now I feel sorry for making that mistake and digging my own grave by bringing all of them to England. I'm naturally a helper and well-wisher, but my decision proved wrong as they weren't the right people and never appreciated my help. I gave them a chance to improve themselves and have a better life, but they deliberately spoiled everything. Young, innocent children lost their mother, which was very painful for them. The whole miserable ordeal precipitated very bad name as well as humiliation, degradation, and suffering to my good family and their innocent children because of two ignorant and stubborn people and bad relatives.

My uncle Lekh Chand was a good man. His blind love for me cost me very dearly at later stage. He died young and left two children. My father did everything he could to make their lives more comfortable and successful by giving them his land and property, but they got spoiled and failed in everything. They both had children, and one was quite promising in his studies. I saw some light for their survival and supported him all the way through college and America. After getting his visa to America, he and his father used primitive magic to fool me, and my eyes were opened. He took everything for granted. After reaching America, he virtually disappeared and proved an overwhelming disillusionment to me. Another surprise was that over time, he grew rich and became a formidable opponent to me. He succeeded in double-crossing people and became a qualified cheater. He was an opportunist who had no real grounding in basic convictions.

Good luck to him. To me, it's goodness over evil and love over hate, just a sting by another cockroach. Sometimes I shout to my good uncle, why did he produce such cockroaches? His grandson, after all his education, marriage, and establishment in America, showed his true dirty colors and character. He proved he is dirt and more vicious than most others and succeeded in his devious plans. He had no humanity and no humility. An educated man without character and humility is more dangerous than a beast, and he proved it. This silly man forgot that God was watching him, and one day he'll pay for his sins.

CHAPTER THIRTY SIX

AFTER RETIREMENT
2001

I didn't have a pension plan, but I was entitled to Social Security benefits, which were good enough to survive in America. Now I was free, and my wife loved to go to Scotland and India to see her friends and relatives. We traveled a lot for three or four years, until she was diagnosed with cancer and passed away in Glasgow in September 2005. There was no sense in blaming myself or her; it was God's will. I was shattered, grief-stricken. She was a very good wife, companion, and responsible mother, but she was no more. She was completely gone, and without her, I felt dead.

All my children and grandchildren traveled to Glasgow from America to pay homage and to prepare their beloved for the final journey. They didn't want me to stay in Glasgow alone, so they made sure that I sold the house in Glasgow before we returned to America. I'd spent fifty-five happy years with my wife, but now I was completely lost and depressed, and it was affecting my health. My desolation after her death was incurable. My children had lost their mother and they couldn't afford to lose their father. They were worried, and I was aware that they had no other reliable relatives and would be very lonely and lost without me.

My daughter, Raksha Devi, knew very well that I loved to travel to see the world's historic landmarks and national treasures. She suggested we go see some places for a change, and I agreed. I started traveling with her, and sometimes without her, to various places like American national parks and popular cities. I didn't get tired easily, and I traveled extensively to Europe, Canada, India, and various parts of America until I was exhausted and satisfied. The months of December, January, and February were very cold in Milwaukee, so I bought a one- bedroom house in warm, sunny Florida, near Disney World. I spent the cold winter months in Florida. I kept that place for ten years and traveled to all the state's important places and cities: Miami, Tampa, Orlando, Cape Canaveral, etc., and its beautiful beaches. Then I felt lonely there and maintaining the house was costly, so I sold it.

When I was in Florida, I saw a big rack of books outside a bookstore. These books were on sale at a reduced price or clearance. I found a book about how to write memoirs and I bought it and started reading it to get some knowledge. In the meantime, the hospital in Milwaukee offered me a job, but I refused. Then they asked me to work on the weekends, and I turned that down because it involved a lot of responsibility and I wanted to have the pleasure of sleeping and waking on my own free will without worrying about work. I wanted to enjoy my life and relax.

I had some beautiful bushes in the backyard of my house in Milwaukee, and in the front, I had evergreen shrubs. I love flowers and greenery. Gardening isn't just good for Mother Earth, it's also beneficial for our health. Gardening is a great activity for any age.

One November day I visited a nursery nearby, and they wanted to get rid of some rosebushes and other plants. Seeing that they were cheap, I bought some, removed some snow from the ground in the freezing climate and dug some holes to plant them. The next summer, they all bloomed with beautiful colors and I didn't lose any plants. Gardening is a big job, and I was getting good exercise by getting down on my knees and standing back up at the age of eighty. I was also getting fresh air and sunshine most of the day. I never got tired of watering, trimming, weeding, and feeding the plants. It was worth the time I spent in my backyard. I made sure I could see the beautiful flowers through all my big windows throughout the summer months. Primroses, crocuses and other early flowering plants like daffodils and tulips refreshed me and soothed my mind after the long, exhausting winter months.

As the weather was changing and turning warmer, more plants and shrubs were blooming, turning the big backyard of my house into a multicolored park. This was my favorite and most deliberate attempt to embrace nature and enjoy the fragrances and textures throughout the summer months. I believed the green grass and scenic outlook would fuel amazing health and adventure to help me live my best life. Life is an exciting journey, and I'm in the driver's seat and must be very careful to make the best of it.

In the evening when it was dark, I came in to eat dinner. I cooked at home or my daughter brought something to eat. When I was in the mood, I watched good shows on television that enriched my life, listened to soothing and pleasant songs to boost my health and well-being, or rested, and sometimes I liked to write or read.

The whole idea was to keep away from bad habits and the bigoted people who gave me trouble and humiliated me all my life. Thank God I'm living in a good residential area where no Hindus, Sikhs, or Muslims live. Like in Scotland, I've enjoyed the company of my American neighbors, who are very helpful and generous. I want to tell my countrymen that I'm not anti-Muslim, anti-Hindu, or anti-Sikh. I'm above all of that. I just can't forget the pain they all caused me with their harmful traditions and customs, so I decided not to give them a chance to see me to humiliate me. From the Hindu, Sikh, and Muslim societies, I got nothing but pain and humiliation, but from Americans, I get love and affection. I'm not antisocial; I love to socialize, but I have no tolerance for drama, stupidity, and fake people who pretend they're high- or super-caste, better than others, and insult and degrade others.

Throughout my life I had to overcome my share of health issues: The depression I endured during my schooling years due to Brahmanism, caste discrimination, and hatred. The dangerous swelling of my throat and neck due to severe tooth decay. A lucky escape from drowning at New Hampshire's beautiful beach. Hospital admissions in Milwaukee due to high blood pressure and regular dialysis for kidney disease. I think the credit for my escapes from death and disease goes to my lifestyle, my belief in God, and my good genes. These account for much of my longevity, as does the companionship of my children and my wife when she was alive.

Another shocking and overwhelming story worth mentioning is that in 2006, I failed some health tests and I was sent to the hospital by my primary doctor for heart catheterization or ballooning. But the surgeon at the hospital told me that I had to go for bypass surgery as all my arteries were full of cholesterol. My daughter Raksha Devi was accompanying me and was fearful about this dangerous major surgery. I was upset as well. The date for surgery was set and four or five assisting doctors were introduced to me within minutes.

In the meantime, news about my heart surgery spread and my eldest daughter Kamlesh, who was employed as a secretary to a research doctor in Philadelphia, asked for a month of leave to spend time with me. There was a picture of me standing very near a waterfall in Yellowstone national park on her desk that I'd sent her from Wyoming when I visited the waterfall there. The doctor immediately told my daughter that I didn't need heart surgery if the person in the picture was me. Anyone who could go down seven hundred feet and then climb back to the surface wasn't sick, he said. The doctor had been to those falls and he knew how difficult they were to climb. He advised my daughter to tell me to cancel the surgery, and I did. Later I got a second opinion from a Pakistani cardiologist. He checked my skin and body from top to bottom, changed my medicine, and advised me to walk for forty-five minutes daily. The surgeon and his team of assistants told me I wouldn't survive long, that I was a ticking time bomb. It's been fourteen years, and I'm living a happy life with my children, grandchildren, and great grandchildren. So please, always get a second opinion from a good doctor before you allow a greedy one to ruin your body.

Life is a good thing. I'm grateful to have been given so much of it, and I want more. I always thank the Almighty for sustaining me, keeping me happy, and letting me do my duties as a simple, humble, true, and compassionate human being. I believe I have only one life to live and I want to live a natural life happily at home. My house is in a very good location, only walking distance to shops and restaurants. The hospital is only two miles away in case I want to see my primary doctor or my cardiologist. I have a good sidewalk for short walks in the morning. For relaxing, I have a hammock and a daybed, my favorite things. I have a place to nap in the backyard where hummingbirds buzz overhead. For mental comfort, I'm surrounded by all those who know and love me. My children and grandchildren are very sincere, and they come and go as they please. They wash my dishes, clean my house, and keep my company.

I get dialysis treatment to clean my blood at a clinic and all the nurses, technicians, and other members are very friendly and helpful. The nurses check my weight and vitals twice and warn me if I have any deficiencies. I keep an eye on my blood pressure and let the nurses know if it's a little high or low. I ensure that my blood moves quickly through the tubes and my body, and I believe this process removes all the sticky fat and cholesterol, a cause of heart failure, from my veins. Hence, life seems secure, comfortable, and healthy from all angles, and I see no reason not to stick around for a few more years or longer. So, this is my America and I love America. I now pass it on to my children, grandchildren, and great grandchildren, and to yours, so they will always know what it is like in America where people are free.

Top: My grandchildren at Neil's wedding
Bottom Left: My children and I on Father's Day
Bottom Right: Anita's MBA Graduation (2013)

CHAPTER THIRTY SEVEN

MY DREAMS AND UNFULFILLED DREAMS

Life is full of dreams. We all have them, both rich and poor. Dreams may be fulfilled or not, but it's good to have dreams to bring into reality. Studies have proven that people with dreams are happier, healthier, and live richer lives.

There are many stories about people who dared to dream big, discussed every possibility, and acted. Each of them had a dream that came with daunting challenges. They kept their focus on the path ahead and achieved success. I've seen a lot of people rise out of poverty due to hard work and understanding. Sometimes it gets discouraging and uncomfortable, it may cause pain, and it can leave one disheartened and bewildered.

The harsh fact of life is that sometimes we're striving endlessly toward the impossible. Mahatma Gandhi wanted to keep India united, but it ended up being divided between India and Pakistan because of enmity between Hindus and Muslims. Pakistan dreamed for a long time of flying its flag in Delhi, but that dream was shattered after three battles with India. Germany dreamed of a place in the sun but failed after fighting two great wars.

AN ONWARD JOURNEY

Many mountaineers have the ultimate dream of conquering Mount Everest, and so many have died on the way to the top without fulfilling that dream. I had a friend who talked about one day going to America. His greatest dream was to settle here. He came, but he ended up in a prison cell in Los Angeles, and that was the story of his life.

We all, in some way, build dreams, and the struggle is always there. My father dreamed of raising his two nephews and turning them into good, successful human beings as he had promised his dying brother. He took great care of them and sincerely hoped to see his dear brother in his children. He did everything he could, but these two nephews started listening to the wrong neighbors and turned against him. My father died brokenhearted and left it to me to look after them. His dream of making his nephews better people was shattered. They were uneducated, cunning, and failed in everything. Like my father, I loved my uncle and I was very sincere to him. I tried to help and support his children and grandchildren as much as humanly possible. I helped them go to college and settle in America so they would have a better life. I may have made them rich, but they weren't rich in values like my uncle, who was honest, kind, and responsible, a good person. I still feel that I was unable to fulfill my promise to my father.

Dr. Ambedkar wanted to change the damaging customs and traditions of Hindu society, but his dream was shattered by orthodox Hindus and others who refused to lift the yoke from the shoulders of women and poor people. In disgust, he resigned his post.

For millions of poor people and untouchables, life is

like a barbarous prison in India, created by the high-caste society and its old rules and traditions. They live under the yoke of imperialism. They live in despair. They're wrapped in deep darkness created by high-caste Brahman priests' mythology and madness. They're denied education and knowledge, but knowledge is power. They have no power and they have no dreams. They find no path to follow and they neither dream nor act. They're forced to do dirty, menial jobs, and high-caste societies live on them and starve them. I was the victim of the same circumstances as the upper caste denied me my basic rights and didn't treat me as an equal, but I tried very hard to reach my goals. As time passed, I embraced my inner resilience and treated life's challenges as opportunities to grow stronger and thrive.

Since my school days, I dreamed of being treated equally, without prejudice. I dreamed of higher degree in education. I dreamed of earning enough money to live lavishly and happily. I dreamed of being a good and honest man. I dreamed of benefiting my country and my community, so my life wouldn't be lived in vain. I tried to give my life to serve and help others, so it wouldn't be wasted. I was loaded with dreams, but sometimes we become so disheartened and helpless that we find it difficult to fulfill our dreams because we depend on others. We must face the facts: not all dreams come true. There was no opportunity to live my dreams in India, so I decided to leave the country and eventually chose to come to America, where I've fulfilled most of my dreams. America has given me all I wanted. America has made me happy. Thank you, America.

The biggest and most difficult challenge I embraced was education, specifically my endeavor to educate myself. Without education, there was no good path to survival for me anywhere. I was very thirsty for knowledge. Again, as the saying goes, "where there is a will, there is a way," and I am a great believer in God although I am not a religious temple goer. My desire and efforts were there, but I believe it was God's will that I went to the UK against all odds. He straightened the way for me and laid the foundation of my education and a life of honor, integrity, and respect. When I became a father, I was frightened about what sort of life and future I would offer my innocent children in the cruel and obstinate society of Hindus and Sikhs in Punjab. By the grace of the Almighty, I have made all my dreams come true as my children are well educated and doing very useful jobs. It was difficult and uncomfortable, but it was worth it to achieve happiness and satisfaction in the future. It was the fulfillment of an oath and a dream that one day I would, with God's help, free myself, my family, and future generations from that evil.

I struggled hard, and my struggles paid off. Today I live among my best American friends. They never ask me which country or religion I belong to, which is a persistent curse among Indian and Pakistani people. I've fulfilled the dreams of my school days. I gained education and experience here and helped many other poor people come to the United Kingdom and the United States so they could have better lives. I helped many gain further education, which was a big aim of my life. I helped educate my children and grandchildren to higher levels and I'm so proud of them. I accepted all kinds of challenges and succeeded in ways that weren't possible in India.

The big dream I had from my school days was to

help my villagers, and for that, I did everything. I studied leather science and technology in the world's best prestigious school in London and prepared myself to go back to my home in India and help my village, but this dream didn't materialize because things in India turned against me. I couldn't see a clear path to success due to political problems and a lack of reliable siblings and relatives. The future of my children and grandchildren and their safety was also a big factor, so this dream of helping my villagers was shattered. Other than this failure, I've fulfilled all my dreams by coming to America, and it's a perpetual regret that my own brothers and sisters, relatives and countrymen made me suffer due to ignorance, bad traditions, and greed. Life is beautiful; life is a dream; life is a challenge. Don't waste it in idle gossip and give your best. Always remember that God helps those who help themselves.

AN ONWARD JOURNEY

SELECTED BIBLIOGRAPHY

Many books, TV shows, and magazines guided me in my writing process. The following are some of the books that have shaped my ideas and made a positive impact on my writing. They have served as precious tools I needed to make my dreams a reality and have transformed my personal experiences and perceptions. Some articles in useful magazines spiced up and enlivened my writing and helped keep me in a highly creative mode.

Adams, Caroline Joy. *The Power to Write: A Writing Workshop in a Book.* Barnes & Noble, 2004.

Ambedkar, Bhimrao Ramji. *Annihilation of Caste: The Annotated Critical Edition.* Verso, 2014.

Anand, Mulk Raj, and E. M. Forster. *Untouchable.* Penguin, 2001.

Fischer, Louis. *The Life of Mahatma Gandhi.* Harper and Row, 1983.

Gandhi, Mohandas K. *An Autobiography, or, The Story of My Experiments with Truth.* Translated by

Mahadev H. Desai. Ahmedabad, India: Navajivan Publishing House, 2016.

Keer, Dhananjay. *Dr. Ambedkar: Life and Mission.* Popular Prakashan, 2016.

King, Martin Luther, Jr., and Clayborne Carson. *The Autobiography of Martin Luther King, Jr.* New York: Intellectual Properties Management in association with Warner Books, 1998.

Majumdar, R. C., H. C. Raychaudhuri, and Kalikinkar Datta. *An Advanced History of India.* Macmillan, 1946.

Nehru, Jawaharlal. *Jawaharlal Nehru: An Autobiography.* Oxford University Press, 1936.

Spear, Percival. *India: A Modern History.* Ann Arbor, MI: University of Michigan, 1961.

Tutu, Desmond. *Dream: The Words and Inspiration of Martin Luther King, Jr.* Blue Mountain Arts, 2007.

Yousafzai, Malala, and Christina Lamb. *I Am Malala: The Girl Who Stood up for Education and Was Shot by the Taliban.* Phoenix, 2014.

Zinsser, William Knowlton. *Writing about Your Life.* Marlowe, 2005.

Zinsser, William. *On Writing Well.* Marlowe, Harper Paperbacks, 2013.

Lastly, a book that I have been carrying with me since my college days in the 1950s called *Rama College Composition.*

END NOTES

[1] R. M. Majumdar, H. C. Raychaudhuri, and Kalikinkar Datta, An Advanced History of India (Publisher Location: Macmillan, 1946).

[2] Percival Spear, India: A Modern History (Ann Arbor, MI: University of Michigan, 1961).

[3] Tutu, Desmond. Dream: The Words and Inspiration of Martin Luther King, Jr. Blue Mountain Arts, 2007.

AN ONWARD JOURNEY